Reflections for Peace of Mind

Reflections for Peace of Mind

365 Meditations for the Year

compiled and written by

Maurice Nassan

Christian Classics, Inc.

Westminster, Maryland 1988

ISBN 0–87061–147–X

First published in
Great Britain 1987 by
Sheed & Ward, Ltd.
First published in U.S.A.
1988 by Christian Classics, Inc.

LIBRARY OF CONGRESS CATALOG CARD
  NUMBER: 88-070302

Preface

This book, as its title indicates, is intended to be a tranquilliser, a spiritual sedative and above all an inspiration to the reader. It covers a wide range of subjects, some composed by the compiler, others by well-known authors both in poetic and prose form. The book can be used as a thought for the day or be opened at random. There is plenty to interest the reader. The passages have been kept short. They should be read slowly so as to give time for their message to sink in.

> What is life if full of care
> We have no time to stand and stare?

> Human nature is like a pool of water. Cast a stone therein, it goes rough and broken; stir it, it becomes foul; give it peace, let it rest, and it will reflect the face of the heavens which lie over it.

January

1 *The New Year*

A traveller in France asked a peasant working in the fields how far it was to Carcassonne. 'How far it is to Carcassonne, Sir, I do not know; but that this is the road to Carcassonne of that I am sure.'

Christians know that they are on the right road to the Carcassonne of their desires but how far it is they do not know. Nor do they know what dangers, troubles, joys or sorrows lie ahead. They cannot 'look into the seeds of time and say which grain will grow and which will not'. There is no gypsy with a crystal ball to foretell their future. And it is just as well that this is so. It would not add to our happiness and would detract from our faith and confidence in God. The beginning of the year is a time for looking forward with faith and determination. Someone has said 'hats off to the past; coats off to the future'. That is quite a good motto for the beginning of the year.

2 *Looking both Ways*

January is named after the Roman god Janus; the god with two faces. In Roman times his name was given to many doorways and arches, some of which were detached ceremonial buildings used for the setting out of a party and especially for the departure of an army. His faces looked two ways, one backward and one forward. This is an apt symbol for us at the doorway of a new year when we tend to look back at past achievements and experiences and look forward with hope that the future will be better. The forward look is much better than the backward. If we are continually dreaming of the past, nursing injuries or sorrowing over misfortunes, it is a sign that we are growing old and have lost the zest of life. Best of all is to live in the present. Our success or failures in the coming year will depend largely upon how we use each moment of the present time.

3 *Grief and Joy*

It is the great mystery of human life that old grief passes gradually into quiet tender joy. The mild serenity of age takes the place of the riotous blood of youth. I bless the rising sun each day, and, as before my heart sings to meet it, but now I love even more its setting, its long slanting rays and the soft, tender, gentle memories that come with them, the dear images from the whole of my long happy life – and over all the Divine Truth, softening, reconciling, forgiving. My life is ending and I know that well, but every day that is left to me I feel how my earthly life is in touch with a new infinite unknown, but approaching life, the nearness of which sets my soul quivering with rapture, my mind glowing and my heart weeping with joy.

The Brothers Karamazov
FEDOR MIKHAILOVICH DOSTOEVSKY 1821–1881

4 *Sunshine*

Begin today to walk the path which alone is gain;
In the sunshine, as the sunshine, calm, contented and
blessed, envying no one, railing not, repining not;

Receiving the message of the patient trees and herbs, and
  of the creatures of the earth, and the stars above;
Possessing all within thyself, with showers of beauties
  and blessings every moment – to scatter again to others
  with free hand;
Neither hurrying nor slackening, but sure of thy great
  and glorious destiny, walk thou –
And presently all around thee shall thou see the
  similitude of him whom thou seekest;
He shall send a multitude of messengers in advance to
  cheer thee on thy way.

EDWARD CARPENTER 1844–1929

5 *Noise*

There is no doubt that the twentieth century holds the record for noise. There are a greater variety of noises today
than there have ever been and they are not only mechanical
ones. The noises coming from the mass media are louder
than ever. The television screen, the radio, magazines and
newspapers pour out their sound of voices telling us what
is good for us, giving us advice on how to live, filling our
imaginations with all kinds of irrelevances. The danger is
that these loud voices deaden our ears to the one voice we
should listen to, the one voice that gives us the best advice
on how to live. We can so easily be beguiled by the be-
witching sounds coming from Vanity Fair. We must remember that Christ speaks with the voice of God. We
cannot hear it unless we are persons of goodwill and are
willing to listen.

6 The Search for Truth

The Magi story is one of mystery and mysticism, symbolic of that striving after truth which has been the mainspring of so much human endeavour. It is the function of wisdom to seek the truth and these wise scholars were endowed, not only with human learning, but also with that supernatural insight which enabled them to recognise truth itself hidden away in a poor cottage in a distant land. Scripture, speaking of wisdom says: 'It is an infinite treasure to men and they that possess it become the friends of God.' This wisdom is not the same as keenness of intellect. Simple shepherds as well as learned scholars became God's friends; both were accustomed to silence and the stars. Both responded to God's message of welcome and both recognised him who contains all the treasures of wisdom and knowledge.

7 The Star

Against the blackness of the night the Magi saw a star. For them it was no ordinary phenomenon. It was light shining out of darkness, a symbol of hope. No doubt they had read the Jewish scriptures and so knew the prophecy of Isaiah about a star that was to arise in Israel. They had the insight to recognise that it was a true prophecy. 'We have seen his star in the East', they said. For them it was a light illuminating a dark past; it was the finger of God pointing the way to the truth. That star was to prove a new dawn for the Gentiles so that when those wise men set out on their journey the hopes of all the Gentiles rode with them. From now on the truth was not to be hidden or disclosed to a chosen race; it was to be there for all men to seek and find.

8 *Night and Day*

Someone has written an imaginary poem about how frightened Adam must have been when he saw the sun disappear for the first time ending the light of day. It was Adam's first darkness, his first night. It was not until he learned that day would come again and no night was endless that his peace of soul returned. So, the poem goes on, it should be with us. We have to learn that however dark and full of trouble life may be, the light is near. Christ once said to his friends 'let not your hearts be troubled, believe in God and believe also in me'. How many have found peace in the light of Christ in the most desperate situations. The poet wrote in prayer:

> Be near me when my light is low;
> When the blood creeps and the nerves prick
> And tingle; and the heart is sick,
> And all the wheels of being low.

9 *Beauteous Evening*

> It is a beauteous evening, calm and free,
> The holy time is quiet as a nun
> Breathless with adoration, the broad sun

Is sinking down in its tranquillity;
The gentleness of heaven broods o'er the sea:
Listen! the mighty being is awake,
And doth with his eternal motion make
A sound like thunder – everlastingly.
Dear child! dear girl! that walkest with me here,
If thou appear untouched by solemn thought,
Thy nature is not therefore less divine:
Thou liest in Abraham's bosom all the year;
And worshippest at the temple's inner shrine,
God being with thee when we know it not.

WILLIAM WORDSWORTH 1770–1850

10 *Solitude and Retirement*

What are the sorrows of other people to us, and what are their joy? Something we may be touched indeed with by the power of sympathy, and a secret turn of the affections; but all the solid reflection is directed towards ourselves. Our meditations are all solitude in perfection; our passions are all exercised in retirement; we love, we hate, we covet, we enjoy, all in privacy and solitude. All that we communicate of those things to any other is but for their assistance in the pursuit of our desires; the end is at home; the enjoyment, the contemplation, is all solitude and retirement; it is for ourselves we enjoy, and for ourselves we suffer.

Robinson Crusoe DANIEL DEFOE 1660–1731

11 *The Cross*

The cross is the answer to the mystery of suffering. The cross itself is an enigma. God's embracement of pain as an expression of infinite love is beyond our capacity for understanding. But at least we can see that suffering can be a way of love and that love can transform pain to make it both bearable and valuable. Thus the cross becomes a liberating and purifying force. It strips a person of pettiness and imparts a largeness of soul and a sympathetic understanding of the pain of others. There was darkness over the earth when Christ died. But he did not die alone. The darkness and death were shared. There was a companionship of pain. And when the darkness gave way to light the light also shone for all. For if we die with Christ we also rise with him.

12 *Cana*

The visit that Christ made to the little village of Cana to attend a marriage feast was only one of countless such visits. For when two people kneel at the altar to plight their troth to one another, Christ is truly present as he was at Cana. In fact he is present in a more intimate way. He sets his seal upon the marriage, imparting his sacramental grace and uniting it with bonds that no human power can tear asunder. He is a true partner to the marriage, offering his personal aid to make it a success and to enable it to meet the challenge of life. Christ comes to those who marry in a union like that of himself with the Church. 'Husbands love your wives', said St Paul 'as Christ loved the Church and delivered himself up for it so that he might sanctify it.' The water of Cana was turned into wine, so also the natural element in marriage is transformed by Christ into something more precious and desirable.

13 *The Sound of the Sea*

There are many sounds in the world today that did not exist at the time of Christ but there is one sound that has existed since the dawn of creation and which will continue to exist as long as the earth lasts. It is the sound of waves breaking on a shore. Peter heard that sound by the sea of Galilee just as we might hear it at Brighton or Blackpool. To us it most likely speaks of holidays but to Peter it meant long nights of toil; it meant his livelihood. At least it meant that until the day came when he heard the voice of the Master: 'Come and I will make you fishers of men.' 'Come', the voice was compelling – yet the sound of the sea still beat in his ears urging him to stay. It was hard to leave what had been so familiar to him since childhood yet the Master's voice prevailed. There are times in the lives of all of us when we must leave familiar sounds and sights we have grown to love. We must try and see the providence of God at work and follow without vain regrets.

14 *Worry*

The First World War song asks: 'What's the use of worrying?' and it adds: 'It never was worth while'. If considered calmly and dispassionately this is true. Worry adds nothing to one's comfort and adds a great deal to one's troubles. Someone has said 'worry is interest paid on trouble before it falls due'. One must be clear about the meaning of the word 'worry'. It is not the same thing as concern. A policeman, for example, should be concerned to the extent of taking wise precautions when he is going into a dark alley where there may be a murderer. But he should not worry, otherwise the alley will become peopled with imaginary killers and he will be useless as a policeman. Imagination can be the friend of worry. It may present a picture of gloom and doom like Mrs Harris's words to Mrs Gamp: 'O Sairey, Sairey, little do we know wot lays afore us.' Christ gave the remedy for peace of heart when he told us to have complete trust in the providence of God.

15 *The Bargain*

My true love hath my heart, and I have his,
By just exchange, one for the other given.
I hold his dear, and mine he cannot miss,
There never was a better bargain driven.
His heart in me keeps me and him in one,
My heart in him his thoughts and senses guides;
He loves my heart, for once it was his own,
I cherish his, because in me it bides.
His heart his wound received from my sight,
My heart was wounded with his wounded heart;
For as from me on him his hurt did light,
So still methought in me his hurt did smart.
Both equal hurt, in this change sought our bliss;
My true love hath my heart and I have his.

SIR PHILIP SYDNEY 1554–1586

16 *Stars in a Thousand Years*

If a man would be alone, let him look at the stars. The rays that come from those heavenly worlds will separate between him and what he touches. One might think the atmosphere was made transparent with this design to give man, in the heavenly bodies, the perpetual presence of the sublime. Seen in the streets of cities, how great they are!

If the stars should appear one night in a thousand years, how would men believe, and adore, and preserve for many generations, the remembrance of the city of God which had been shown? But every night come out these envoys of beauty, and light the universe with their admonishing smile.

RALPH WALDO EMERSON 1803–1882

17 *Self-portrait* 

What kind of self-portrait hangs in the gallery of our minds? Is it possible to step back and look at it and see the 'I' in 'me' and get a perfect likeness? Can we reproduce ourselves in our minds 'warts and all'? No one achieves this to perfection. Does one recognise one's own voice when it is recorded? Does one really know one's own face? If one's double walked down the street would one recognise him as such? If, then, that is true of one's physical features how much more true must it be of one's own character. Do we really know what sort of person we are? Of course there are many things we do know about ourselves. We know the broad outlines of our self-portrait but few of us, if any, know the more subtle chiaroscuros and lineaments. The trouble is we get in our own light. Often we see just what we would like to see or expect to see. A little humility would be helpful when we paint our own portrait.

18 *A Good-night*

Close now thine eyes, and rest secure;
Thy soul is safe enough; thy body sure;
He that loves thee, he that keeps
And guards thee, never slumbers, never sleeps.
The smiling conscience in a sleeping breast
Has only peace, has only rest:
The music and the mirth of kings
Are all but very discords, when she sings:
Then close thine eyes and rest secure;
No sleep so sweet as thine, no rest so sure.

FRANCIS QUARLES 1592–1644

19 *Loneliness*

In small bed-sitters, in second or third floor backs, in little terraced houses or in giant apartment blocks live a whole host of lonely people. Most of them are poor (the rich usually have friends or at least companionship); many of them are disabled in some way so that they are anchored to their rooms. They eke out their existence as best they may on a small pension or tiny savings. Their relations are dead or far away, and they have no friends.

What is the worst of woes that wait on age?
What stamps the wrinkles deeper on the brow?
To view each loved one blotted from life's page.
And be alone on earth as I am now.

Such words of the poet can be applied to many in our cities. In their old age they have become withdrawn within themselves, isolated, impervious to the busy life about them, with only their dreams of past achievements to keep them company. 'It is not good for man to be alone' says Scripture. Perhaps we can help.

20 *Loveless*

Francis Bacon wrote: 'A crowd is not company and faces but a gallery of pictures and talk but a tinkling cymbal where there is no love.' We all like good company and the laughter and talk of friends. There are those who have nothing of these things and there is much that can be done for them. A ride in the country or to the sea may mean a great deal to a lonely person. An hour's chat with perhaps a little present of some tea or tobacco can bring great pleasure. Old people like to talk about the past and it gives them joy to have a good and ready listener. This comforting of the lonely and those deprived of love is a splendid apostleship. It needs tact and self-denial. For the Christian the comforting of those people is the comforting of Christ who identifies himself with them.

21 *Present Happiness*

'Distance lends enchantment to the view.' How very true this is in human psychology. When life is difficult we tend to look back and think how much easier things were or we look forward to some future time and think how much easier life will be once our present troubles have departed. The poet Shelley wrote: 'We look before and after and sigh for what is not.' How rosy the past can look. 'Those were the days', we murmur. The prisoner of Chillon chained to his prison floor drags his shackles to the small window where he can catch a glimpse of the beauty of the outside world. He can see the distant hills and lake and longs to be free to enjoy them. He no doubt wonders how anybody can be discontented in such surroundings, free to wander under the open sky and to feel the warmth of the sun. Yet there can be self-deception in this. If at some future date he was released from his chains he would certainly have the happiness of freedom but would it last? Other troubles might easily arise. The happiest people are those who try and make the most of the present, who are not forever looking back over their shoulders or looking forward to better things.

22 *The Age of Automation*

Rudyard Kipling in his poem *The Secret of the Machines* wrote:

Though our smoke may hide the heavens from our eyes,
It will vanish and the stars will shine again,
Because – for all our power and weight and size –
we are nothing more than children of your brain.

From out of the tiny mass of grey jelly of the human brain spring enormous factories filled with complicated machinery, amid whose hum and whirl millions live their lives. These machines are certainly in one sense the children of the brain but often they become its master. It is not always true that the smoke 'will vanish and the stars will shine again' in many peoples' lives. The world of the machine holds them in its grip, clouding their vision. Its 'power and weight and size' have so taken hold of them as to crush their true manhood. Trade and money and products have become the be-all and end-all of their existence. There is no time to look at the stars. God, to use St Augustine's sentiments, cannot give them anything because their hands are full.

23 *O! Come Quickly*

Never weather-beaten sail more willingly bent to shore,
Never tired pilgrim's limbs affected slumber more,
Than my weary spright now longs to fly out of my
    troubled breast.
O! Come quickly, sweetest Lord, and take my soul to
    rest.

Ever blooming are the joys of Heaven's high Paradise.
Cold age deafs not there our ears, nor vapour dims our
    eyes;
Glory there the sun outshines, whose beams the blessed
    only see,
O! Come quickly, glorious Lord, and raise my spright to
    thee.

THOMAS CAMPION 1507–1620

24 *A Creed*

Life appears to me to be too short to be spent in nursing animosity or registering wrongs. We are one and all burdened with faults in this world, but the time will come when, I trust, we shall put them off in putting off our corruptible bodies; when debasement and sin will fall from us and only the spark will remain, the impalpable principle of life and thought, pure as when it left the Creator to inspire the creature. Whence it came, it will return, perhaps to pass through gradations of glory.

It is a creed in which I delight, to which I cling. It makes Eternity a rest, a home; not a terror and an abyss. With this creed revenge never worries my heart; degradation never too deeply disgusts me, injustice never crushes me too low. I live in calm, looking to the end.

CHARLOTTE BRONTE 1816–1855

25 *The Madman in the House*

Someone has labelled imagination 'that madman in the house'. Clearly, this cannot mean that wonderful faculty of the mind which is the source of poetic fancy and inventive genius. Nor could it mean that power we all have of picturing absent objects and people. What is obviously meant is that type of imagination which plays us false. Shakespeare wrote:

The lunatic, the lover and the poet
Are of imagination all compact.

It is the lunatic imagination that the writer had in mind, the kind that causes neurosis in its various forms, which invents falsehoods dressed up in truth. All kinds of anxieties exist in that type of imagination and have no foundation in the world of reality. A child in the dark will imagine he sees ghosts and goblins and in the same way an adult can become the prey of dreadful fears of the unknown. One remedy is not to think too much about oneself. The less egocentric we are the less will we be bothered by 'the madman in the house'.

26 *Imagination*

Imagination can play havoc with human relationships. A passing remark, a look, a thoughtless action can spark off all kinds of dark suspicions and dislikes even though no evil purpose was intended. Persecution mania is the direct consequence of a perverted imagination; it takes on various forms and brings with it great unhappiness and loss of friendships. What is the remedy for this lunatic imagination? The best thing is to tie the fellow up in the house, thus keeping him under control. One simply must not let one's imagination run wild about one's neighbour. Think of his good points and not just of his weaknesses. Prayer is a great help here if it is properly entered into. It helps us to have a clear vision of the world and it purifies our unworthiness. Above all it makes us look outward towards God and not inward towards ourselves.

27 *The Scolding by a Wife*

When he was in the Tower, and there had continued a good while, his said wife obtained licence to see him. Who, at the first coming, like a simple ignorant woman, and somewhat worldly too, with this manner of salutation bluntly saluted him. 'What the goodyear, Master More,' quoth she, 'I marvel that you that have been always hitherto taken for so wise a man, will now so play the fool to lie here in this close, filthy prison, and be content thus to be shut up among mice and rats, when you might be abroad at your liberty, with the favour and goodwill both of the king and his counsel, if you would do as all the bishops and best learned of this realm have done. And seeing you have at Chelsea a right fair house, your library, your books, your gallery, your garden, your orchard and all other necessaries so handsome about you, where you might in the company of me your wife, your children and your household, be merry, I muse what a God's name you mean here thus fondly to tarry!'

After he had quietly heard her, with a cheerful countenance he said unto her: 'I pray thee, good Mistress Alice, tell me one thing.' 'What is that?' quoth she. 'Is not this house,' quoth he, 'as nigh heaven as mine own?' To whom she, after her accustomed homely fashion, not liking such talk, answered: 'Tilly vally, tilly vally.'

The Life and Death of Thomas More
NICHOLAS HARPSFIELD 1519–1575

28 *Constant Love*

Let me not to the marriage of true minds
Admit impediments. Love is not love
Which alters when it alteration finds,
Or bends with the remover to remove,
O, no! It is an ever-fixed mark,
That looks on tempests and is never shaken;
It is the star to every wand'ring bark,
Whose worth's unknown, although his height be taken.
Love's not Time's fool, though rosy lips and cheeks
Within his bending sickle's compass come;
Love alters not with his brief hours and weeks,
But bears it out even to the edge of doom.
If this be error, and upon me prov'd,
I never writ, nor no man ever lov'd.

WILLIAM SHAKESPEARE 1564–1616

29 *Inner Beauty*

To a person with spiritual insight the world has an inner beauty which is reflected in its outer form: the sunset is more than its chemical brilliance, flowers more lovely than their shape and colour, all nature more splendid than its changing pageantry. He penetrates beyond their superficialities to discover 'a beauty ever ancient, ever new' sustaining them and imparting to them a radiance of its own. Where there is beauty there is mystery because beauty excites wonder. The key to the mystery is the Spirit of God who first gave beauty to the world when it was void and shapeless. Outward beauty is the Spirit's invitation to look deeper and see the source from which all beauty flows.

30 *False Beauty*

There is a false seductive beauty which creates an illusion of attractiveness and can so easily end in frustration and misery. Christ described the beauty of a fig tree as an image of unfaithfulness. He used the image of white sepulchres as an image of inner corruption. The bible is full of images of this fatal beauty. It suggests that it was this fatal beauty that brought disaster upon the world. Our first parents saw that the forbidden fruit was 'good to eat and pleasing to the eye and delightful to behold'. They were seduced by its beauty so that it became a means of corruption. And yet it is true to say that there is no such thing as false beauty, only perverted beauty, beauty used for false ends. All beauty is the splendour of truth. God is the author of beauty. Robert Browning wrote:

> The beauty and the wonder and the power,
> The shapes of things, their colours, lights and shades,
> Changes, surprises, – and God made it all.

31 *The Spirit of Beauty*

Francis Bacon said: 'In all beauty there is some strangeness of proportion.' Beauty, like a diamond, has many facets; it exists in numerous shapes and forms. It has both body and soul in the sense that it has a material and a spiritual expression. Both are creations of that Spirit of God who gave harmonious expression to the world. At His coming sunlight burst upon a dark universe and the moon and the stars shone against the black velvet of the night. The 'strangeness of proportion' of beauty arises from the continual presence of the Spirit endowing everything with a miraculous splendour. The whole world is incandescent with his fire. D. H. Lawrence wrote: 'In the seed of the dandelion, as it floats with its little umbrella of hair, sits the Holy Ghost in tiny compass. The Holy Ghost is that which holds the light and the dark, the day and the night, the wet and the sunny united in one little clue.' No doubt Lawrence was not thinking of the Holy Ghost as Christians think of Him but he certainly was admirably expressing the result of His presence.

February

1 *Purification*

February takes its name from a Latin word meaning purification. The month was named after a pagan Roman festival celebrated on the fifteenth day of the month. This was
the Lupercalia or the feast day of the god Lupercus. Goats
and a dog were sacrificed on that day. The celebrants ran
round the old city walls striking all whom they met with
thongs cut from the skins of the slaughtered animals. These
blows were reputed to preserve women from sterility. For
the Christian this has become the month of the Purification
when the parents of Christ complied with the Jewish law
which ordained that forty days after the birth of a first male
child it must be taken to the temple to be presented to the
Lord.

2 *The Mother brings Her Child to God*

Deep in the warm vale the village is sleeping,
Sleeping the firs on the bleak rock above;
Nought wakes, save grateful hearts, silently creeping
Up to their Lord in the might of their love.

What thou hast given to me, Lord, here I bring thee,
Odour and light and the magic of gold;
Feet which must follow thee, lips which must sing thee,
Limbs which must ache for thee ere they grow old.

What thou hast given to me, Lord, here I tender,

Life of mine own life, the fruit of my love;
Take him, yet leave him me, till I shall render
Count of the precious charge, kneeling above.

CHARLES KINGSLEY 1819–1875

3 *The Dawn of Faith*

To stand on a hillside just before the dawn and watch the gradual illumination of the countryside can be an inspiring experience. Up from below the horizon comes the first gleams of the light of the approaching dawn. The surroundings are revealed faintly in the grey light. Then comes the rising sun flooding the fields with gold. And now what was dark and impossible to see stands out in full perspective. So it is with the dawn of faith. We see it realised in the apostle Thomas. His mind was darkened by the death of Christ. A dead body on a cross was for him the death of faith. His whole world was in impenetrable darkness until the Light of the World appeared and brought illumination and understanding. The actual sight of Christ and the touch of his wounds brought Thomas to his knees in sorrow to make his act of faith.

4 *The Vision of Faith*

Christ pointed out that we must be like the converted Thomas but without his advantage of sight. We are to remain in the dark in respect of His presence and yet to have the vision of faith to know that He is near. We are not to see but we are to believe. This is not always easy. There can be dark moments in our lives when Christ seems far away and we seem to be on our own. Like Thomas we see only a dead Christ. But this is our testing time. We are to accept with all our being that Christ is not dead but is alive and risen and is taking an interest in our lives. We should repeat to ourselves in those dark moments the words of Christ: 'Blessed are they who have not seen but believe.'

5 *The Peace of Christ*

Christ promised to give peace to his followers – a peace 'not as the world gives do I give it to you'. What is the difference between worldly peace and the peace of Christ? The former peace is largely negative and external, a peace arising from the end of a war or a quarrel, a peace made through a treaty or agreement. The peace of Christ is deep down in the heart of a person. It is like the calm in the depth of the sea which nothing can disturb. It can exist amid all the bustling activities of life and also amid trials and suffering. Christ himself experienced this peace all during his passion. It was a peace that came from his union with the Father. This too is the basis of the peace which Christ offers. It arises from the knowledge and understanding of the presence of God within us. This creates within us an area of strength and calm which the noises of the world cannot dispel.

6 *Peacemakers*

We won't find God amid noise and restlessness. We need to pray to Him to bring Him into our lives and those of others. Mother Teresa of Calcutta wrote: 'So let us radiate the peace of God and so light his light and extinguish in the world and in the hearts of men all hatred and love for power.' Christ said: 'Blessed are the peacemakers for they shall be called sons of God.' As Christians we must both create peace within ourselves and also bring peace into the lives of others. The 23rd psalm is a prayer for peace and well worth using:

> He guides me along the right path;
> He is true to His name.
> If I should walk in the valley of darkness
>   no evil would I fear.
> You are there with your crook and your staff;
>   with these you give me comfort.

7 *Born of the Spirit*

In the book of Genesis we are told that when God made man He breathed into his nostrils the breath of life and so man became a living being. He became a spiritual being, vibrant with the divine, taking on the image and likeness of God. Hence, right from the beginning man was under the influence of the Spirit. It was Christ who made this clear when He revealed the nature and being of the Spirit. He said that a man cannot enter the kingdom of God unless he is born of the Spirit. He showed us that it is possible to deny the Spirit and so destroy the image of God within us. The importance for us is to open ourselves out to His influence and power. That Spirit, who in the beginning moved over the darkness, chaos and barrenness and brought forth light and harmony and life, will do the same in the little cosmos of our self if we pray earnestly to him.

8 *The Comforter*

The Holy Spirit is our 'Comforter' and our 'Advocate'. He enlightens and inspires us. He lives in the depth of our being as a temple 'sanctifies us into a dwelling place for God'. The Spirit is the source of our spiritual life. We cannot call upon God without the Spirit. St Paul wrote: 'God's love has been poured into our hearts through the Holy Spirit which has been given to us.' He is the Spirit of love. All true love in whatever form it takes, love of knowledge, love of art, love in marriage, love of mothers for their children, is the infinite breath of God upon our lives. The Holy Spirit is personified love. He is the consummation of the union of Father and Son. His creative breath gave birth to the world and thus the world was conceived in love. This breath continues to inspire love and impart its force. For all human beings are in some way under the power of the Spirit: even those who refuse love cannot altogether evade it, for without Him they are nothing.

9 *The Human Christ*

After Christ had risen from the dead He did not become a disembodied spirit. He remained human. When He manifested himself to His apostles by the lakeside He showed His very human side. He clearly took a delight in springing a surprise upon them when He stood on the beach and watched the approaching boat with its emptiness of fish. He enjoyed working the miracle so that they could enjoy an abundance. He loved to prepare breakfast for them and to serve them with bread and cooked fish. The whole affair made them silent during the meal and Christ no doubt enjoyed that too, understanding their feelings so well. It is good for us to think of the human side of Christ. It is a consolation to us to know that He can think and feel like us and to know also that the human in Him is there to draw us to the divine.

10 *Early Childhood*

Our birth is but a sleep and a forgetting:
The soul that rises with us, our life's star,
Hath had elsewhere its setting,
And cometh from afar:
Not in entire forgetfulness,
And not in utter nakedness,
But trailing clouds of glory do we come
From God, who is our home:
Heaven lies about us in our infancy!
Shades of the prison-house begin to close
Upon the growing boy,

But he beholds the light, and whence it flows,
He sees it in his joy;
The Youth, who daily farther from the east
Must travel, still is Nature's Priest,
And by the vision splendid
Is on his way attended;
At length the Man perceives it die away
And fade into the light of common day.
Intimations of Immortality WILLIAM WORDSWORTH
1770–1850

11 *Self-pity*

Prison walls are not the only form of confinement. There are people who are wholly immured within their own skins. They are narrow and stunted and emotionally hidebound. They do not know what real joy is and they go about blinkered, without sympathy or fellow-feeling.

Sometimes their gaoler is suffering, either mental or physical. He keeps them enclosed in a welter of self-pity. They seem to shut themselves off completely from the outside world and cover themselves with sharp protective casing 'like quills upon the fretful porcupine'. There are others who withdraw themselves inward through some imagined or even real injury. They place themselves 'in Coventry' and become embittered and joyless. The Spirit of God is the key which opens all these prison doors. St Paul tells us 'where the Spirit of the Lord is, there is liberty'. Where the Spirit of Love is there can be no room for bitterness or egoism, no withdrawal into the self nor blindness to the existence of others' needs.

12 *A Nightmare World*

Imagine a world without hope or the spirit of joy. Such a world would be a nightmare. In its most oppressive form it would be the world of Winston Smith in George Orwell's satire *1984*: 'All competing pleasures will be destroyed. But always there will be the intoxication of power. Always, at every moment, there will be the thrill of victory, the sensation of trampling on an enemy, who is helpless. If you want a picture of the future, imagine a foot stamping on a human face – for ever.' This century has seen such worlds in miniature – in the horrors of concentration camps and in cells where interrogations, drugs, inhuman treatment have been inflicted on men in the pursuit of some vile ideology. Such ugly joyless worlds are created by men who lust for power without love. They do not listen or care to listen to the song which the Spirit longs to sing in the hearts of men.

13 *Religious Growth*

There is the curious view of some people that in religious matters a child's mind should be allowed to lie fallow until it develops sufficient intellectual perception to choose its own form of belief. Such people do not think that what is left uncultivated soon grows wild. What on earth are the poor adolescents supposed to do? Must they study all the chief religions of the world and, having sized them all up, decide where the truth is to be found? Will study alone do this? Surely it is common sense that if a child is brought up with no religion the odds are that it will not acquire one; or one at least that will be an inspiration to its life. A good parent who is convinced of the truth of his own faith will insist, and rightly so, upon passing on that truth to his children. The children don't question the right of the parents to do so. Later, the children will grow up and examine the reasonableness of what they have been taught.

14 *The Pep-pill Age*

Happy pills, pep-pills, tranquillisers – how many go down human throats every day? Their numbers run into millions. They have become the antidotes to anxiety, to complexes, fear-fixations, work-tensions, worry in its multiple forms. They are the recognised remedy for heart-aches, headaches and most of the other aches which afflict the human body and soul. They are the tonic for the neurotic, the narcotic for the sleepless. Tranquillisers certainly have their place in curing human troubles and anxieties but their indiscriminate use should have no place at all. There must be a time for go-slow in human life; and it is in this that the remedy for many human ills should be found rather than in the chemist's shop.

> What is life, if full of care
> We have no time to stand and stare?

Let us pause sometimes in our daily toil and allow the psychotherapy of prayer to bring us peace.

15 *A Father's Advice*

Advice from his father to the, then, schoolboy Sir Philip Sidney: 'Be courteous of behaviour and affable to all men; there is nothing that winneth so much, with so little cost. Seldom drink wine, yet sometimes do; lest, being forced on a sudden to drink, it should inflame you. Delight to be cleanly; it shall make you graceful in each company. Let your mirth be ever void of all scurrility and biting words, for a wound given by a word is harder to be cured than that given by a sword. Above all things tell no untruth, not even in trifles, for there cannot be a greater reproach to a gentleman than to be accounted a liar. Your mother and I send you our blessing and Almighty God grant you his, nourish you with his fear, guide you with his grace, and make you a good servant to your prince and country.'

16 *The Soul in all Things*

There lives and works
A soul in all things, and that soul is God.
The beauties of the wilderness are his,
That make so gay the solitary place,
Where no eye sees them. And the fairer forms,
That cultivation glories in, are his.
He sets the bright procession on its way,
And marshals all the order of the year;
He marks the bounds which Winter may not pass,
And blunts his pointed fury; in its case,
Russet and rude, folds up the tender germ,
Uninjured, with inimitable art;

And, ere one flowing season fades and dies,
Designs the blooming wonders of the next.
The Task WILLIAM COWPER 1731–1800

17 *The Stolen Godhead*

Once upon a time, or rather at the birth of Time, when the gods were so new that they had no names, and Man was still damp from the clay of the pit whence he had been digged, Man claimed that he, too, was in some sort a god. The gods weighed his evidence and decided that Man's claim was good.

Having conceded Man's claims the legend goes on that they came by stealth and stole away this godhead with intent to hide it where Man should never find it again. But this was not so easy. If they put it anywhere on earth the gods foresaw that Man would leave no stone unturned till he had recovered it. If they concealed it among themselves they feared Man might batter his way up even to the skies.

And while they were all there at a stand, the wisest of the gods said: 'I know. Give it to me.' He closed his hand upon the tiny, unstable light of Man's stolen godhead, and when that great hand opened again the light was gone.' All is well,' said Brahm, 'I have hidden it where Man will never dream of looking for it. I have hidden it inside Man himself.'

RUDYARD KIPLING 1865–1936

18 *A Mind Content*

Sweet are the thoughts that savour of content;
The quiet mind is richer than a crown;
Sweet are the nights in careless slumber spent;
The poor estate scorns fortune's angry frown:
Such sweet content, such minds, such sleep, such bliss,
Beggars enjoy, when princes oft do miss.
The homely house that harbours quiet rest;
The cottage that affords no pride nor care;
The mean that 'grees with country music best;
The sweet consort of mirth and music's fare;
Obscured life sets down a type of bliss:
A mind content both crown and kingdom is.

ROBERT GREENE 1560–1592

19 *The Power of the Mind*

Over three hundred years ago the blind poet John Milton expressed a vital truth:

The mind in its own place, and in itself
Can make a Heaven of Hell, a Hell of Heaven.

These words are an echo of those spoken centuries before by Marcus Aurelius, the philosopher who ruled the Roman empire: 'Our life is what our thoughts make us.' Thus if we think happy thoughts we become happy people; if miserable thoughts we become miserable people. Now is it beyond human willpower to channel one's thoughts in the right direction. Of course there are occasions when a person is overwhelmed by some personal disaster but this should not remain a permanent state otherwise Hell will ensue. Mental powers have a tremendous effect upon physical well-being. If one is to face life successfully and happily one must at times make positive efforts to think courageous thoughts.

20 *Credulity*

The famous American showman Barnum once gave in London a renowned lecture on mermaids. He exhibited a couple which he had found (so he said) on a remote island in the Pacific. The mermaids were really monkeys on which Barnum had fitted a salmon's tail but the public were willing to accept the maxim that 'seeing is believing'. This incident demonstrates how credulous some people can be. It is true that this happened in Queen Victoria's reign but people can be just as simple in our modern age. There are those today who only accept the maxim 'seeing is believing'. They will not accept as true what their senses cannot reveal to them. To accept the existence of mermaids is foolish, but it is just as foolish to flout the evidence of reason and say that all the marvellous harmony in the world, all its beauty, its life, all the wonder of human personality are self-explanatory and in no way depend upon a creative power. It is the fool who says there is no God.

21 *Time*

The landlord said: 'Time, Gentlemen, Time.' In a corner of the inn sat a dead man at a table with an empty mug at his side and a few scraps of unfinished food on a plate. It was closing time. Time for all to leave, but this man had left before all the others. Time is a strange phenomenon. The only part of it we can call our own is that split second known as 'now'. It is in that split second that our fate is decided: 'Now is the acceptable time; now is the day of salvation.' We can look back at the past and look forward to the future but we can only live and die in the present. The 'now' is vastly more important for the Christian than for the unbeliever. For the latter it is the moment for drinking the cup of pleasure; for the former it is the means of prolonging happiness for ever. We must live for God in the present in order that our future may be assured.

22 *The Harvest Day*

It may not be our lot to wield
The sickle in the ripened field;
Not ours to hear, on Summer eves,
The reaper's song among the sheaves.
Yet where our duty's task is wrought
In unison with God's great thought,
The near and future blend in one,
And whatso'er is willed is done,
And where this life the utmost span,
The only end and aim of man
Better the toil of fields like these
Than waking dream and slothful ease.
But life, though falling like our grain,
Like that revives and springs again;
And early called, how blest are they
Who wait in heaven their harvest day.
JOHN GREENLEAF WHITTIER 1807–1892

23 *Resentment*

She was an old lady. She toiled painfully up the steep stairs
to the railway station. Someone said to her: 'You find the
stairs difficult?' 'Yes,' she replied, 'I don't come here much
now but once I used to climb them regularly and easily but
now I find them very hard. I resent it.' We would all save
ourselves a lot of anxiety and care if we did not resent what
we cannot avoid. We should all try and learn to cooperate
with the inevitable. We should see in the inevitable the
working of God's will for us. God's providence is gov-
erning our lives and when circumstances arise in our lives
which are unavoidable our reaction should be as far as
possible one of calm acceptance and not of resentment.
This is not easy, it is something that requires the help of
prayer.

24 *Providence*

Ruskin is reported as having said: 'You knock a man into a
ditch and then you tell him to remain content in the position in which Providence has placed him. That is modern
Christianity.' There is an echo in those words of the com-
munist cry that religion is the opium of the people; the idea
that authority makes use of religion to keep employees
subservient to those who are exploiting them. This, of
course, is specious nonsense. Christianity does not tell
people that they are to be content with their station in life
and should never try and improve themselves. What it does
say is, that, given a certain set of circumstances (such as
being in a ditch), it is always possible and right to make use

of them in God's service whilst at the same time doing one's best to get rid of them (by climbing out of the ditch). God has created human beings to live on this earth and has given them certain talents and powers. It is part of their service of God to make use of these gifts to their best advantage.

25 *True Freedom*

There is a strange misconception that freedom means absence of restraint. Yet freedom can only be obtained by obedience to law. Without law it degenerates into license. For example, people are only free to use their cars on the roads if they obey the highway code; if they refuse, the scrap merchant will soon be collecting the car and the ambulance its occupants. Disobedience to law results in slavery; obedience in liberty. Disobedience to the laws of fire or drugs can bring death. The whole of one's day only becomes free if one obeys laws during it. If one does not obey cookery laws one goes without one's breakfast. If one does not obey employment laws one goes without one's job. And what is true of the world about him is also true of the inner life of a human being. If he revolts against the normal purposes of his life, he degenerates and becomes less human. God has made man in a certain way and he is not free to act in other ways without harming himself.

26 *Fears*

All of us at times have felt our stomach full of butterflies when we were about to face some event which we feared. Fear is a normal reaction to the unpleasant and the dangerous. But fear in the plural can have a very different meaning. A famous American general took as his motto: 'Never take counsel of your fears.' Kipling said: 'Of all the liars in the world, sometimes the worst are your own fears.' True courage has a moral quality. It has its springs in the mind and its exercise in the will. The most fearful are the most courageous when they overcome their fears. 'More life may trickle out of a man through thought than through a gaping wound', wrote Kipling. The sensitive and the imaginative person is more prone to give way to fear than others and hence has greater possibilities of courage. Courage is not necessarily a virtue; it can be one under the inspiration of the Spirit.

27 *Human Clams*

There are some people who are never open to conviction. They have made up their minds and that is the end of it. They are case-hardened like clams, nursing their opinions within an impenetrable shell of obstinacy. Like the clams which adhere to rocks by the force of their own suction, such people hold to their own way of thinking by some adhesive power generated from within. Even when the truth is staring them in the face they will hold to its contrary. All of us can be guilty of this obstinacy to some degree in our spiritual lives. Perhaps we are meditating on some passage in the New Testament when the truth of Christ's words stand out clear and challenging. They are unpalatable; they fill us with a feeling of discomfort. So we misinterpret them; give them a meaning we would like them to have; shrug off their true meaning. It takes a rock to break a clam's shell. It takes courage to open ourselves out to the truth.

28 *Brother Ass*

When Francis of Assisi called his body Brother Ass he did not mean that his body was evil. He meant that because of sin the perfect harmony that should exist between body and spirit in a person has been unsettled so that the body can be a drag on the soul. There is a constant civil war going on inside human beings between the forces of the spirit and those of the sensual life. St Paul describes it as being waged between the law of the mind and the law of the members. The pagan Ovid wrote: 'I see and approve the better things of life, the worst things I follow.' And the Greek philosopher Plato described personality as a charioteer driving two headstrong horses, one of the animals is appetite (or instinct), the other is spirit. The driver, who is reason, has the greatest difficulty in keeping both horses heading in the right direction. St Paul wrote: 'If you live according to the flesh you shall die; but if by the Spirit you mortify the deeds of the flesh you shall live.'

March

R.P.M.—D

1 *Living Water*

Beneath one of the vast deserts of Australia an unlimited supply of water has been discovered, sufficient to make a part of the desert fertile with flowers and trees and crops. Without water there can be no growth; everything becomes stunted and withers. Water is essential for life. Hence men are always striving to irrigate dry lands. They build their cities on the banks of rivers and create vast reservoirs to preserve water to feed industry and the needs of the population. It was natural then to use water as a figure of spiritual refreshment. Thus the prophetic voice of Isaiah said:

> I shall pour water on the thirsty ground
> and streams on the dry land;
> I will pour my spirit upon your descendants
> and my blessing on your offspring.

It was of this living spiritual water that Christ spoke to the Samaritan woman. 'If you knew the gift of God ... you would have asked of him, and he would have given you living water.'

2 *Love's Message*

In a sermon, shortly before his death by assassination, Martin Luther King quoted a poem by Alma Androzzo:

> If I can help somebody as I pass along
> If I can cheer somebody with a word or song,

If I can show somebody he is trav'ling wrong,
Then my living shall not be in vain.

Those words express in poetic form what Christ said: 'Let your light so shine before men that they may see your good works and give glory to your Father in heaven.' The hippies had a much-used phrase: 'I've got to do my own thing.' The Christian interpretation of that saying is, in the last words of the poem, 'to spread love's message as the Master taught.' The Christian cannot be self-contained. He must let his good works provide hope and faith and love in others so that, in turn, they will glorify God.

3 *The Last Day*

Dressed in flowing white robes 26 people sat tense and silent in an upper room in a London house. Leader of the group was a middle-aged solicitor. He had given up practising law after experiencing what he called an amazing series of dreams. He claimed that it had been revealed to him that the world would come to an end on 23 July 1887 at 3.00 p.m. He gained twenty-five believers and they bought a house in North London. On the fatal day they were gathered in a room, watching the clock ticking towards the fateful hour. 3.00 p.m. came and went. It wasn't the end of the world but it was the end of the solicitor. After his followers had left in bewilderment he shot himself. There have been many dire predictions about the date for the end of the world, but dates come and go and the world goes on. Christ tells us 'of that day or that hour no one knows, not even the angels in heaven, nor the Son, but only the Father.' Christ does not want us to play the guessing game. What He wants is for us to be prepared for the end.

4 Two Temples

Some forty years after Christ's death the Roman armies attacked Jerusalem and, after one of the most terrible and horrifying sieges in history, left it a blackened ruin. The lovely temple, the pride and joy of every Jew, was razed to the ground and the surrounding hills were covered with the crosses of crucified men. This destruction is used in the Gospels as a picture of the end of the world. It will be plain then, that goodness has overcome evil. Amid the dark ruin of the world will shine forth the majesty and greatness of Him to whom 'all power is given in heaven and on earth'. He who went through the darkness and pain of Calvary to a glorious resurrection will manifest His victory over evil. Just as from the ruins of the temple and Jerusalem a new temple 'not made with hands' and a new Jerusalem would arise, so out of the world's end would come a finer existence.

5 The Best Seller

The Bible is the world's best seller. It can be read in almost every language. All its seventy-three books have an underlying unity. All are the story of God and man. The book is centred upon a little country no larger than Wales. In that country stupendous events took place which will have an impact on the world until the end of time. But the Bible is, above all, God's revelation of himself to men. It begins with God's revelation of Himself through creation and continued with further revelation when He called Abraham telling him to leave his home and go into a land which He would show him. Abraham's obedience was the starting point of a new race which was to be called the people of God. St Paul wrote: 'All Scripture is inspired by God, it is profitable to teach, to reprove, to correct, to instruct in justice.' St Paul had the Old Testament in mind, but this is true of all Scriptures.

6 *The Word of God*

The Bible is the only book in the world which involves God in its authorship. This does not mean that God put into the minds of those who wrote it the actual words and style. The Bible is not a miraculous work that has fallen out of Heaven. It is a work written under the inspiration of the Holy Spirit. He moved the sacred writers to write, and helped them while they wrote, to make it 'profitable to teach, to reprove, to correct, to instruct in justice'. He did not interfere with their style of writing but they wrote under His guidance. Because of this the books of the Bible are graceful and if they are read with devotion the grace will flow out of them to the reader. Christ, who is the centre of the Bible, spoke words loaded with grace and it is our task to release its flow through our devotion and prayer.

7 *Marvel of Marvels*

Marvel of marvels if I myself shall behold
With mine own eyes my King in his city of gold;
Where the least of lambs is spotless white in the field,
Where the least and last of saints in spotless white is
   stoled,

Where the dimmest head beyond a moon is aureoled.
O Saints, my beloved, now mouldering to mould in the
    mould,
Shall I see you lift your heads, see your cerements
    unrolled,
See with these very eyes? Who now in darkness and cold
Tremble for the midnight cry, the rapture, the tale
    untold,
'The Bridegroom cometh, cometh, his Bride to enfold.'

Cold it is, my beloved, since your funeral bell was tolled:
Cold it is, O my King, how cold alone in the wold.
CHRISTINA GEORGINA ROSSETTI 1830–1894

8 *The Secret of Humanity*

A wonderful fact to reflect upon, that every human creature is constituted to be that profound secret and mystery
to every other. A solemn consideration, when I enter a
great city by night, that every one of those darkly clustered
houses encloses its own secret; that every room in every
one of them encloses its own secret; that every beating
heart in the hundreds of thousands of breasts there, is, in
some of its imaginings, a secret to the heart nearest it! ... In
any of the burial-places of this city through which I pass, is
there a sleeper more inscrutable than its busy inhabitants
are, in their innermost personality, to me, or than I am to
them?
A Tale of Two Cities CHARLES DICKENS 1812–1870

9 *The Fish-hooks*

Mark Twain spoke of a certain Mrs Watson who, when he was a boy, told him that whatever he prayed for he would get. Once, he said, he had a fish-line but no hooks. He prayed three or four times for the hooks without result. When he asked Mrs Watson for an explanation she said he was a fool but she did not explain why. No doubt we would consider it very pleasant to get all the things we might pray for. We could have as much money as we wanted and all kinds of comforts. Suppose every wish were granted; would we be better off? The Greeks had a proverb that when the gods were angry with a person they gave him all he wanted. What kind of character would we have if we got everything we wanted without effort? Some of the things might well prove harmful in themselves. God wants us to struggle and work and face the challenge of life with its ups and downs and so win our spurs for the world to come. Our prayers must contain the faith that they are answered but not always the way we would like them to be answered.

10 *Listening to God*

Prayer is our only real means of communicating with God and one good way of doing this is by listening to Him. We can listen to Him through His words in Scripture or we can sit back in silence and think of His presence in our lives. Listening involves silence. This is a silence which is not merely cessation of noise, but a silence deep down in one's heart. If one is full of distracting influences one cannot listen. There must be an atmosphere of peace if the word of God is to be heard. God entered our world when 'all things were in quiet silence'. This is the way He enters our life. We mustn't be so 'busy about many things' that we have no time for quiet contemplation. If we have goodwill and try our best to listen to God we can be sure to get a response from Him even though we do not hear His voice.

11 *Reverential Fear*

In *The Wind in the Willows* Rat and Mole are on their way to the island where Pan was living. Mole, shaking with fear, whispers: 'Rat, are you afraid?' 'Afraid', replied Rat, his eyes shining with unutterable love, 'Afraid? of him? O never, never. And yet, and yet – O Mole I am afraid.' Fear is of different kinds. There is the fear that makes cowards and the fear which is of the essence of courage since courage consists in overcoming it. Then there is the Rat and Mole type of fear which has a basis of reverence and admiration springing from the sense of the presence of power and greatness. This fear should be experienced by all of us. Scripture calls it the beginning of wisdom. The more we contemplate the nature of God, His immensity, His majesty, holiness and infinite love, the more we should recognise our own insignificance. We should not, of course, be afraid of God. Our fear should arise out of our reverence and even out of our love.

12 *Freedom from Want*

A cartoon in a newspaper showed a monk walking through a large department store. He was surrounded by all kinds of splendid goods, jewels, clothes and expensive ornaments. On his face was a large smile. The caption read: 'Freedom from Want'. That is a good illustration of what the wise Roman Seneca said: 'If you would make a man happy, do not add to his possessions, but subtract from the sum of his desires.' There is a real peace and happiness in being independent of things. This does not mean that we should not want to possess them; it means that we should not want them to possess us. Christ expressed this by saying: 'Blessed are the poor in spirit for theirs is the kingdom of Heaven.' Poverty of spirit thus results in the riches of a kingdom.

13 *The Origin of Things*

When Charles Darwin's *Origin of Species* was published it caused a certain amount of disquiet. Ralph Vaughan Williams, when a small boy, asked his mother what it meant. She replied: 'The Bible says that God made the world in six days. Great Uncle Charles thinks it took much longer; but we need not worry about it, for it is equally wonderful either way.' The Bible tells us that 'in the beginning' God made our world. It did not make itself. It is not, as some unbeliever stated: 'A mudpie made in the dark by two blind children, Matter and Force.' The Bible tells us that the world was made through the Word of God. When Abraham Lincoln was only nineteen he said: 'I never behold the stars that I do not feel that I am looking in the face of God. I can see how it might be possible for a man to look down upon the earth and be an atheist, but I cannot conceive how he could look up into the heavens and say there is no God.'

14 *Divinity Within*

Now for my life, it is a miracle of thirty years which to relate were not a history but a piece of poetry, and would sound to common ears like a fable. For the world, I count it not an inn but a hospital, and a place not to live but to die in. The world that I regard is myself: it is the microcosm of my own frame that I can cast my eye on; for the other, I use it like my globe, and turn it round sometimes for my recreation. That mass of flesh that circumscribes me limits not my mind. That surface that tells the heavens it hath an end cannot persuade me I have any ... While I study to find out how I am a microcosm, or little world, I find myself something more than the great. There is surely a piece of divinity in us – something that was before the elements, and owes no homage to the sun.'

Religio Medici SIR THOMAS BROWNE 1605–1682

15 *The Spiritual Adventure*

Thomas Carlyle wrote: 'If seen with insight and dramatic imagination every life has elements of romantic biography.' He was no doubt thinking of the power of the novelist or dramatist to make a subject of romance of very ordinary lives. But his words can have another and more profound meaning. They can be seen in the context of man's soul in regard to God. His Spirit of love enters into human lives making them into a spiritual adventure. No longer do they live purely on a material level; there is another life within them which is under the guidance of the Spirit. This does not mean that they despise material things and try and live like 'Little Johnny Head-in-Air'. Their spiritual adventure takes place amid the dust of everyday activities. Life is not a dream. Escapism only creates delusion.

16 *Personality*

God's greatest gift to man is his personality; that in him which makes him unique and capable therefore of receiving unique graces. And because he is unique, the only one out of countless millions, all that he does has its own special quality in the eyes of God. This greatness in man is far more wonderful than any natural marvel such as the Niagara Falls or Mount Everest or any artificial creation such as the sculpture of Michelangelo or the paintings of Raphael. The depth of the personality is the meeting place of God with the individual. It is a place of mystery. This adventure of the soul with God is so mysterious and awe-inspiring that it can only be accepted in the spirit of faith. Through faith the inmost self realises its contact with God, not as something physically felt or capable of worded expression or emotionally perceived but as an awareness accompanied by an inner peace and strength.

17 *The Price of Eternal Happiness*

An artist's brush and canvas and paint are of little value in themselves. It is the use to which they are put that give them their value. If he is a great artist, the painter will fashion out of the paint images which are a beauty and a joy for ever. The pictures, for example, that Fra Angelico painted were extensions of himself. He put himself in some way into the paint; impressed his personality upon it. It was his imagination, skill and keen aesthetic sense that created priceless pictures. All of us have very ordinary materials at our disposal in life but God has made it possible for us to give them divine significance, and hence a worth beyond all price. The ordinary everyday actions of our life are extensions of ourselves and if they spring from a self supernaturalised by the grace of God they lose their ordinariness and become the price of eternal happiness. Thus our life becomes full of meaning. It is not judged by God according to status, intellect or talent; His criterion of judgement is worth.

18 *Consideration*

When I consider how my light is spent
Ere half my days, in this dark world and wide,
And that one talent which is death to hide,
Lodged with me useless, though my soul more bent
To serve therewith my Maker, and present
My true account, lest he returning chide:

Doth God exact day-labour, light denied,
I fondly ask; but patience, to prevent
That murmur, soon replies, God doth not need
Either man's works or his own gifts; who best
Bear his mild yoke, they serve him best; His state
Is kingly; thousands at his bidding speed
And post o'er land and ocean without rest:
They also serve who only stand and wait.

JOHN MILTON 1608–1674

19 *Good News*

Ever since the world began God has been publishing news about Himself. The world itself is the newsprint of God but one must put on the spectacles of faith in order to be able to read it both in its large and small print. But God was not satisfied with this. He wanted to give more details about Himself. So it was that He spoke to men and His spoken word was recorded in Scripture and played back through the ages by the Church which has preserved His message. But even that way was not sufficient for God. He wanted to give still more news about Himself. So it was He sent His Son into the world to become His official inter-preter. So Christ came and spread the good news of God among men, telling them about God's kingdom and how they should enter it and one day see God face to face.

20 *Understanding*

The philosopher and writer Ralph Emerson once, with his son, tried to force a calf into a barn. Emerson got behind the calf and pushed and his son got in front and pulled. But the calf refused to budge. It stiffened its legs and stubbornly remained where it was. An Irish maid saw their difficulty. She had little learning but on this occasion she showed far more wisdom than the learned Emerson. She placed her fingers in some milk and then placed them in the mouth of the calf allowing it to lick them and then she gently drew the calf into the barn. All of us can do with some of that girl's wisdom in our dealings with people. We should not, for example, try and bludgeon them into conforming to our way of thinking. We should do our best to put ourselves in their place, to understand their point of view, find out what they like or dislike.

21 *The Spirit of Man*

The make-up of a human being is a mystery. It is not possible to analyse him or to bottle him. He is far more than his chemistry; that can be analysed – so much lime and sulphur, carbon and iron and water. Break up a person into parts and he is no longer a human being since he is essentially an integration of body and spirit. 'Care I for the limbs, the thews, the stature, bulk and big assemblage of a man? Give me the spirit Master Shallow.' We can all echo those words. What we admire in people and what attracts us to them is not so much their shape or size or weight, it is that mysterious element in them which gives them a unique quality. This is the spirit in them, the core of their personality. No amount of self-analysis can solve it. It is this spirit in them that needs divine guidance to keep the balance between spirit and matter, to quell the civil war which so easily erupts within them.

22 *Victory over Self*

For man to gain victory over himself he needs the partnership of God. Peace on earth comes to those who are God's friends. A man is so easily the centre of tensions. He can become tied by his own desires and whims and he must look beyond himself for release. This was the experience of St Augustine when he wrote: 'I sighed, chained as I was, not by iron, but by my own will stronger than iron.' The self in man is at the heart of the riddle of his existence. That 'I' which is so wayward, which is so apt to poison its own well-springs has the power of turning in upon itself and becoming its own worst enemy. God deliberately made man a mysterious entity, wilful, powerful in intellect, an enigma to himself so that he would have to look for a solution to the puzzle not in himself. God, when he created the riddle of self in man, kept the key to the solution but at the same time revealed that He had the key and would hand it over when man's destiny was fulfilled.

23 *The Mystery of Things*

There is a mixture of clarity and obscurity about things. Light reveals their surfaces, their colour, their shape and their identities. It delves into their chemistry, their intricacies of design and purpose. Yet there is always something elusive about them. Neither mind, sight or imagination can penetrate their depth and ultimate nature. Their essence and existence defies scientific analysis and philosophical enquiry cannot exhaust their content. There is a force and energy and subsistent power which remain impenetrable. 'And straight down New Street was Christ College tower. Phil Tombs looked at the tower, Tom tower, closing the vista of New Street ... "Funny how everything solid expresses something that isn't solid at all."' So spoke a character in a novel by J. M. Stewart. Always behind the tangible solidity of things is the intangible which is somehow expressed in their structure. What looks so real and impenetrable is a shadow of another reality.

24 *A Universal Presence*

Francis Thompson wrote:

> All things by immortal power
> Near or far
> Hiddenly
> To each other linked are
> That thou canst not stir a flower
> Without troubling of a star.

Radio, television, satellite are proofs of this intercommunion of things. The full scientific reason for this is not apparent but there is a far deeper mystery than the scientific one. It is the mystery arising from a divine essence pervading everything and yet not extended or confined within limits. A universal presence unites all creation – the reality behind the shadow play of everyday phenomena. Everywhere the wisdom, beauty, power of this reality is demonstrated.

25 *Peace amid Turmoil*

The American general George Patton wrote: 'The first Sunday I spent in Normandy was quite an experience. I went to a Catholic field Mass where all of us were armed. As we knelt in the mud in the slight drizzle, we could distinctly hear the roar of guns and the whole sky was filled with 'planes on their way to destruction . . . quite at variance with the teachings of the religion we were practising.'

It is possible to have peace of heart even amid turmoil and destruction. Christ knew that his coming would result in strife but he said to his friends: 'My peace I give you, not as the world gives it to you but as I give it.' This is that peace deep down within us even amid all kinds of tribulations and troubles.

26 *Eternal Beings*

H. G. Wells in his autobiography wrote: 'I realise that Being is surrounded East, South, North and West, above and below, by wonder. Within that frame, like a little house in strange, cold, vast and beautiful scenery is life upon this planet, of which I am a temporary speck and impression.'

In one sense his words are true, life is fleeting, we are here in this world for a relatively short time and are only an insignificant part of it. On the other hand the glory of Christianity reveals that we are not a 'temporary speck'. We are eternal beings with a greatness bestowed upon us by God.

27 *What is Life?*

Many answers have been given to the question 'What is life?' The Old Testament gives a number of answers. It is like grass that springs up in the morning and by evening it withers and fades. It is like a shepherd's tent which he sets up before sunset which he takes down in the morning and all that is left is silence and emptiness. Without Christ there is no real answer to the question. 'Grace and truth' came through Him. 'I have come that you may have life and have it abundantly,' He said. Life is no longer just a shadow or a dream. Christ also said: 'I am the Resurrection and the Life.' With Him we can all rise up to a life without end, a life full of purpose and significance.

28 *Images into Truth*

Sophocles, the Greek dramatist wrote: 'We are nothing else but phantoms as long as we live and empty shadows.' There is a sadness about the view of life of those who do not know the Truth. This is beautifully expressed in the last words attributed to an Indian chief named Crowfoot: 'A little while and I will be gone from among you, whither I cannot tell. From nowhere we come into nowhere we go. What is life? It is a flash of a firefly in the night. It is a breath of a buffalo in the Winter-time. It is as a little shadow that runs across the grass and loses itself in the sunset.'

Cardinal Newman chose as his inscription for his tomb 'From the shadows and the images into Truth'. We know that God has given substance to the shadows and made them significant.

29 *The Death of Wolsey*

He was in his confession the space of an hour. And then Master Kinston came to him and bid him good morrow and asked him how he did. 'Sir', quote he, 'I watch but God's pleasure to render up my poor soul to Him. I pray you have me heartedly commended unto his Royal Majesty and beseech him on my behalf to call to his princely remembrance all matters that have been between us from the beginning; and especially between good Queen Katherine and him, and then shall his Grace's conscience know whether I have offended him or not ... I do assure you I have often kneeled before him, sometimes three hours together, to persuade him from his will and appetite, but could not prevail. And Master Kinston, had I but served God as diligently as I have served His king, He would not have given me over in my grey hairs. But this is the just reward that I must receive for my diligent pains and study, not regarding my service to God, but only to my Prince.

Now began the time to draw near, for he drew his speech at length and his tongue began to fail him ... And then presently the clock struck eight, at which time he gave up the ghost.

The Life and Death of Thomas Wolsey
GEORGE CAVENDISH 1500–1565

30 *In Westminster Abbey*

Mortality, behold and fear,
What a change of flesh is here!
Think how many royal bones
Sleep within this heap of stones;
Here they lie had realms and lands,
Who now want strength to stir their hands;
Where, from their pulpits sealed with dust,
They preach: 'In greatness is no trust.'
Here's an ache sown indeed
With the richest royalest seed
That the earth did e'er suck in
Since the first man died for sin.
Here the bones of birth have cried:
'Though gods they were, as men they died.'

FRANCIS BEAUMONT 1584–1616

31 *A Toothache*

God takes an interest in the smallest troubles of our lives. What seems so trivial in itself becomes quite big when it affects our lives. So it was with the toothache which St Augustine experienced as described in his Confessions. 'When shall I remember all the things that passed in those days of my retirement? But neither have I forgotten, nor will I keep in silence the sharpness of the scourge and the admirable swiftness of Thy mercy. Thou didst then torment me with the toothache, and when it was grown to such height of violence that it made me speechless, it came to my mind to desire all my friends there present that they would pray unto Thee who art the God of all kind health. Immediately as soon as with humble devotion we had bowed our knees, the pain fled away. But what kind of pain was that, and how it went from me? I was much afraid, I confess, O Lord, for in all my life I have never felt the like.'

April

1 *The Month of Spring*

The derivation of the word April is not certain but it probably comes from a Latin word meaning to open because it is the month when buds and flowers begin to open out in the Spring. It is a time when all nature springs to life. The sap rises in the trees, the plants push their green shoots through the soil and hibernating animals come out of their hiding places. A universal resurrection takes place. Winter is the fertilising time of Spring; from what was dead comes new life and vitality. But April is not only the time when nature rises from its long Winter sleep. It is also the time when we commemorate the Lord of Nature's resurrection after the dark Winter's death of his passion. He was the grain of wheat that died, was placed in the earth and did not remain there. On Easter morning He rose to new life and with Him rose the hopes of all mankind.

2 *The Blind Beggar of Bethnal Green*

There was a young girl whose name was Bess and she was very beautiful. Four men wanted to marry her: a knight, a money lender, a merchant and the son of an inn-keeper. She told them that she must first ask her father, the poor blind beggar of Bethnal Green. When they heard this they all slunk away except the knight who went and asked the beggar for the hand of his daughter. The beggar gave his leave and also £3,000 (a lot of money in those days). He also gave Bess £100 for her wedding dress. When the time came for the wedding feast the beggar told the guests who he was. He was of royal blood, the son of a famous man whose name was Simon de Montford. The beggar had disguised himself because he was in hiding from his enemies who wanted to kill him.

No doubt a number of moral conclusions can be drawn from that story.

3 *Free Entertainment*

'What would you not pay to see the sunrise if Nature had not improvidently made it a free entertainment?' There is a good deal of truth in that wise remark. There are many such free entertainments provided for us by God. We do not have to pay to see the loveliness of Nature; even a single blade of grass has beauty for those who have the eyes to see it. Christ said of a flower: 'I tell you that Solomon in all his glory was not clothed like one of these.' And we can look at flowers without paying. The sea, the sky, the countryside contain innumerable objects for our free entertainment. Perhaps we do not appreciate this enough. St James may be of help: 'Every best gift and every perfect gift is from above, coming down from the Father of light with whom there is no change nor shadow of alteration.'

The source of the light is unchanged and unchangeable but the reflection of it makes our world luminous with his presence.

4 *Eternal Destiny*

The mechanism of a human being is designed to enable him to adapt himself to the world in which he lives. His faculties make it possible for him, not only to survive, but also to earn a living, to advance in culture, to become a member of a family and a state and through all this gain security and happiness for himself. But all this is not the ultimate purpose of such a mechanism and should not be considered so – though there are those who think it is and others who act as though it was.

All that goes to make up a human being, his mind and will, his eyes and hands and feet, are designed to reach beyond their immediate practical purpose by giving glory and honour to God. God did not design human beings simply for existence in this world. He had an ultimate purpose in mind that they should have an eternal destiny. Human beings are so made that through their work and energies in this world they give glory to God and so win eternal happiness with him.

5 *Christ and His Father*

Every Christian knows that one cannot picture God in one's imagination. One knows that any representation of Him is bound to be false and whatever idea of Him one has must necessarily contain false notes. On the other hand, every Christian knows that it is possible to be aware of God's presence and to know something of His characteristics, that He is lovable, powerful, wise etc. In this life no man can come face to face with God in His glory. The

Israelites could not even look upon the reflected glory on the countenance of Moses. Yet in the human race there has always been the desire to express the unseen in the seen; a longing to see God in tangible form. Hence men have created perversions – idols to express Him or see Him as sun or moon or stars. It was God Himself who fulfilled their desires by giving them Christ. 'He who sees me sees the Father', He said.

6 *The Violin*

An old battered violin may look very useless and unsightly. It may lie in a shop for years because no-one likes the look of it. But one day, perhaps, a great violin player enters the shop and takes the violin and plays upon it until the whole instrument becomes vibrant with the beauty of sound. Now the violin has great value; the violinist has discovered and revealed its worth by inspiring it with a beauty and greatness which its outward looks belied.

So it is with us and God. By ourselves we are of little value. We are weak and ineffective and ugly with sin but once God takes hold of us, comes and dwells within us, plays upon us with His grace we become vibrant with new life and energy and beauty far beyond what our ordinary nature manifests.

7 *The Image of God*

Why is human personality so valuable in God's eyes? Is it because he is its creator? That is partly the answer but certainly not the complete one. After all God created the birds and plants and the Gospel tells us that people are much more valuable than they are. The answer surely lies in what the book of Genesis tells us, that man was made to the image and likeness of God. God's perfect image is the second person of the Trinity and hence He is the object of God's perfect love. Human beings are made so that they can become replicas, in so far as the limitations of their nature allows, of that second person made man. Hence God loves them in so far as they express this image; in other words, in so far as they live the Christ life. It is Christ then who is the source of our value; His blood and His rise to glory have made us precious in God's eyes.

8 *Heaven*

The Reverend Sydney Smith said that a certain person's idea of Heaven is eating Pâtés de foie gras to the sound of trumpets. Heaven has often been caricatured in the form of harps and damp clouds and strange musical accompaniments but most of the caricaturists do not expect people to take them seriously. On the other hand there is in some peoples' minds the idea that the joy of Heaven consists in a never-ending round of the kind of physical and mental pleasures that we experience on earth. Nothing could be further from the truth. The essence of beatific happiness is to be found only in God and of 'living with Christ'. The mind's function is to search for Truth and it will only find its full satisfaction in the knowledge of Truth Himself. The heart is made to love and only Love Himself will give it perfect joy.

9 *Stillness*

We all need a centre of silence in our being when we pray. We should at times get away from our normal activities. This does not mean that we cannot pray while watching television or washing the dishes; but it does mean that our prayer will not go very deep unless there are times when we meditate in silence and peace. 'Be still and know that I am God', says the psalmist. To be still means not only in our bodily movements but in stillness of the mind. This means trying to keep distracting thoughts away and keeping our mind and heart on God. This at first is not easy. It entails practise and preparation. We must first of all put ourselves in a silent mood and find a place of silence. There is no doubt that this silent meditation does give an inner strength to one's being. God becomes one's strength.

10 *Silence*

Mother Teresa of Calcutta said: 'We need to find God and He cannot be found in noise and restlessness. God is the friend of silence. See how Nature – trees, flowers, grass – grows in silence; see the stars, the moon and sun, how they move in silence. Is not our mission to give God to the poor in the slums? Not a dead God, but a living, loving God. The more we receive in silent prayer, the more we can give in our active life. We need silence to be able to touch souls. The essential thing is not what we say, but what God says to us and through us. All our words will be useless unless they come from within – words which do not give the light of Christ increase the darkness.'

11 *Winter and Spring*

After Winter comes the Spring. Once the ground was frost-bound, choked of flowers and shrubs. The singing of birds was no longer heard and a cold silence gripped the land. But afterwards comes a new world of joy, of light and growth. The whistling of birds is heard and flowers press up through the ground. Said the prophet Isaiah:

> For as the earth makes fresh things grow,
> as a garden makes seeds spring up,
> so will the Lord God cause righteousness and praise
> spring up in the sight of the nations.

The world can be compared to Winter before God's coming to it in human form. His coming was like the Spring. New life was given; a light shone in the darkness a wilderness of sin was made fertile by His grace.

12 *Kindness*

Mother Teresa of Calcutta said: 'Be kind and merciful. Let no-one ever come to you without leaving better and happier. Be the living expression of God's kindness in your eyes, kindness in your smile, kindness in your greeting.' She points out that there are so many who need this kindness, the poor, the lonely, the neglected, the unwanted people for whom nobody has time. St Paul tells us: 'Have that mind which was in Christ Jesus.'

We are to see others the way Christ saw them; try to understand others as He understood them. This means taking a real interest in their lives. Someone has said: 'You can make more friends in two months by becoming interested in other people than you can in two years by trying to get other people interested in you. People are interested in themselves; if we can learn to share that interest, we will make them our friends.

13 *Pride*

George Eliot wrote of a man that he was like the barn-door cock who believed that the sun rose in the morning for the sole reason of hearing him crow. There is something rather ridiculous about a cock crowing on a dung hill, but it is ludicrous to see a human being *fanfaronading* about his miserable conceits. The cock might conceivably have something to crow about; the man has nothing. Pride is the worst of all sins because it is a form of self-idolatry. It is an insult to God since the proud man arrogates to himself the gifts that God has bestowed upon him. Life is far too short for such boasting and conceits. A poet wrote:

> Of all the cocks that greeted dawn today
> How many will be heard a year from now?
> How many preen their feathers on the heap?
> How many strut the yard, how many crow?

14 *Self-control*

Cardinal Vaughan reminiscing about his boyhood said: 'On one occasion when I had shown overmuch relish for some dish, my father reminded me that it was a poor thing to be a slave to any appetite or practice. Blushing to the roots of my hair, I ventured to retaliate saying: "Well, father, how is it that the snuff box is brought to you every day at the end of dinner? You always take a big pinch." For a moment he was silent, then he made me fetch the box, and while in the act of tossing it into the fire he said: "There goes the box and that is the end of that bit of slavery." '

Cardinal Vaughan was emphasising the fact that we must remain captains of our souls. Christ said: 'A man's life does not consist in the abundance of his possessions.' We must always be in command of our possessions and not let them enslave us. Augustine said: 'Love and do what you want.'

15 *The Use of Things*

St Ignatius of Loyola wrote at the beginning of his little book *The Spiritual Exercises*: 'Man has been created to praise, reverence and serve Our Lord God thereby saving his soul. Everything else on earth has been created for man's sake to help him to achieve the purpose for which he has been created. So it follows that man has to use them as far as they help and abstain from them when they hinder his purpose.'

Everything then has both a natural use and a divine use. Everything is there to help us on our way through the world and everything is also there to help us on our way to an eternal life with God. Oscar Wilde described a cynic as a person who knows the price of everything and the value of nothing. There are plenty of people who fit that description. They know the price of things but have no inkling of their hidden value – the power to express the love of God.

R.P.M.—F

16 *Two Seas*

There are two seas in Palestine which are both fed by the River Jordan. They are the Sea of Galilee and the Dead Sea. The former is fresh and fish swim in it and trees grow round it in which birds make their nest. People enjoy walking along its banks. The latter sea, as its name indicates, is a dead sea. The difference between these seas is that the Sea of Galilee receives its waters from the river but does not keep them. For every drop that flows into it, another drop flows out. The other sea, the Dead Sea, keeps every drop it gets. The Sea of Galilee gives and lives; the other sea gives nothing. Those two seas are symbols of two kinds of people. Those like the Sea of Galilee are grateful. They have received so much from God and are ready to give their lives to Him in return. Those like the Dead Sea are selfish, wrapped up in themselves. They do not give themselves either to God or to their neighbour.

17 *The Huge Practical Joke*

There are certain queer times and occasions in this strange affair we call life when a man takes the whole universe for a vast practical joke, though the wit thereof he but dimly discerns, and more than suspects that the joke is at nobody's expense but his own. However, nothing dispirits, and nothing seems worth while disputing. He bolts down all events, all creeds, and beliefs, and persuasions, all hard things visible and invisible, never mind how nobly as an ostrich of potent digestion gobbles down bullets and gun flints. And as for small difficulties and worryings, prospects of sudden disaster, peril of life and limb; all these and death itself seem to him only sly, good-natured hits and jolly punches in the side bestowed by the unseen and unaccountable old joker.

Moby Dick HERMAN MELVILLE 1819–1891

18 *Prayer of St Francis*

Lord make me an instrument of your peace
Where there is hatred let me sow love,
Where there is injury, pardon,
Where there is doubt, faith,
Where there is despair, hope,
Where there is darkness, light,
Where there is sadness, joy.

O Divine Master, grant that I may not so much seek to be consoled as to console; to be understood as to understand; to be loved as to love; for it is in giving that we receive; it is in pardoning that we are pardoned and it is in dying that we are born to eternal life.

19 *The Power of Growth*

An eternal rhythm of life, like a current of fire, runs through the universe; birth and rebirth, death and resurrection form a continual cycle of existence. In Nature life feeds on death. The flowers of one year feed the flowers of the next. Flowers must die in order that others may live. The destruction of one thing is the reconstruction of another. Life, like music has 'a dying fall'; always the law of diminishing returns haunts it. It rises to a peak of intensity then goes into decline to give way to new revelations of existence. Christ was not immune from this law. He used the comparison of a seed to express it. He said: 'Unless a grain of wheat falls to the ground and dies, it remains alone. But if it dies it bears much fruit.' Just as in the dark Winter the seeds in the earth remain lifeless until the Spring brings forth new shoots so Christ in the Winter of His Passion died and was buried and then came forth in the new Springtide of the world.

20 *The Life Force*

The life force in a human being is intense. Its thrust is constantly urging him forward to new enterprises and the conquest of new realms of knowledge. Always he is breaking down a containing shell of knowledge and, chrysalis like, opening out new horizons of experience. Only when the Spirit departs from him does he fail; then civilisations collapse, culture is sterilised.

> You hide your face, they are dismayed;
> you take back your spirit, they die,
> returning to the dust from which they came.
> You send forth your spirit, they are created;
> and you renew the face of the earth.

Always man is endeavouring to 'renew the face of the earth' but this he cannot do without the cooperation of the Spirit.

21 *New Life*

Christ spoke at dead of night to Nicodemus: 'Truly I say to you, unless one is born of water and the Spirit, he cannot enter the kingdom of God.' Out of water, as out of a womb, emerges new life conceived by the Spirit. That Spirit who once 'moved over the waters' of creation and from its dark womb brought forth a multitude of living things now brings new life on a higher plane through 'living water' that will become a spring of water welling up into eternal life. This new life is far more vigorous and cogent than that of the body. It acts like a powerful electric current conveying light and warmth and, though unfelt, it pervades all human activities making the mind perceptive of divine truths and human faculties on fire with divine love.

22 *Watch and Pray*

On D-Day – when the Allies in the Second World War landed in occupied France – they did so at an unexpected time and place. The German commander, Rommel, was on leave at his home; in Germany, Hitler was asleep and was not to be disturbed. Neither expected that the invasion would take place. The weather conditions seemed to prohibit it. They were uncertain where it would happen. Their lack of readiness certainly contributed to their defeat.

Christians are people on the watch. 'Take heed, watch and pray, for you do not know when the time will come,' said Christ. Death is seldom forseeable. Many who have thought themselves to be in the best of health have suddenly died.

Accidents claim many also. If we really believe in what happens after death we would be foolish not to be prepared for it.

23 *Fullness of Time*

'When the fullness of time had come God sent his Son made of a woman, made under the law' wrote St Paul. Fullness of time implies completion – a coming to a head. This was the Springtide in world history, affecting all human affairs. It was a time to which all previous ages moved under the providence of God and from which all subsequent ages would take their momentum. For God had come on earth and submitted himself to the restrictions of time so that we mortals might eventually have the freedom of timelessness. It was an hour in history forged out of the past. The river of time which had had its source in the creative act of God now reached its full flood. For the kingdom of God, which had been repudiated by the human race because of its sinful disobedience, would now be restored in a far more glorious way with Christ as its king.

24 *The Indwelling Presence*

God communicates His inner life to men. He enters into the very depth of their being making it a Holy of Holies. God is love and love manifests itself in the desire for union. The indwelling presence of God in a human personality is an expression of the love of God, of His desire to break down barriers between Himself and men. This immanence of God baffles the mind and imagination. When one thinks of the immensity of God and contrasts it with our puny being it becomes ever more puzzling. What we do know, and it is this that gives dignity and value to our nature, is that God in some mysterious way communicates His life to humanity without destroying its identity. God acts upon a human being in those regions of self which give him his identity so that a special relationship is set up between the self and God.

25 *Spirit of Renewal*

G. K. Chesterton wrote: 'If seeds in the dark earth can turn into such beautiful roses what might not the heart of man become in its long journey towards the stars.' The Holy Spirit is the Spirit of renewal. His wind and fire came upon the apostles on the first Pentecost bringing about a complete change of heart. From being frightened, weak, ignorant of God's ways and the teaching of Christ, they became full of courage, strong and wise. This wind and fire acts upon all Christians. The wind is the breath of God – the word Spirit means breath. And just as at the beginning God breathed upon the dust of the earth and shaped it to His own image, so He continues through His Spirit to make that image closer to the reality.

26 *Nature's Law*

'Tis Nature's law
That none, the meanest of created things,
Of forms created the most vile and brute,
The dullest or most noxious, should exist
Divorced from good – a spirit and pulse of good,
A life and soul, to every mode of being
Inseparably linked. Then be assured
That least of all can aught – that ever owned
The heaven-regarding eye and front sublime
Which man is born to – sink, how'er depressed,
So low as to be scorned without a sin;
Without offence to God cast out of view...

WILLIAM WORDSWORTH 1770–1850

27 *The Light of the World*

St Augustine prayed: 'O God, who in the beginning willed that light should burst forth from the prevailing darkness, say to my poor soul, "let there be light" and my soul shall be filled with light. Without thee I am unable to distinguish between light and darkness, truth and error. It is the absence of thy heavenly light which causes such confusion in the mind and that leads to spiritual blindness and even to the death of the soul.'

Christ is the light of the world. Without him the whole world is dark. He came to illumine every man who comes into the world. Without Him we would be walking in a world of dark mystery, life would have little meaning and our future would be insecure. Christ is the light because He is the Way, the Truth and the Life. He is God's revelation to us of the reason for our existence.

28 *The Darkened Mind*

There are many ways in which minds can grow dark. Prejudice, for example, can cloud our mind so that we see others as in a distorted mirror. This can result in dislike or even hatred. Slogans and propaganda of various kinds heard on television or radio or read in newspapers can easily obscure the truth. 'Let your light shine before men,' said Christ.

The light of which He is speaking is that divine insight manifesting itself in action. Our minds can also be darkened by our own image, an image which becomes so gargantuan that it casts its shadow on the whole world around us. Our eyes should not be mirrors but windows of clear glass so that we have a true vision of things. 'God is our light,' said a saint, 'the further the soul strays away from God the deeper it goes into darkness.'

It is this light of God that helps us to see life in its true perspective.

29 *The Nightmare*

A man had a nightmare. He was walking down a street and people kept on coming up to him and treating him as though he was someone else. He cried out: 'I'm Tom

Jones.' But the people simply laughed and went on treating him as someone else.

It is a terrible thing to lose one's identity. We all want to be treated as individuals with our own personality. Our danger lies, not in loss of identity, that is impossible, but in its realisation; in becoming so part of a nondescript crowd that we become identified with it. We can so become caught up in a mechanistic culture that we become cogs in a machine and conditioned by its superficial trivialities. Mechanisation, automation, the general standardisation of life tend to produce the 'organisational man' rather than the individual. The solution is not to try and break away from one's immediate environment, this is normally impossible, but to humanise oneself through a corresponding spiritual life. Christ said: 'Seek first the Kingdom of Heaven and all these things will be added unto you.'

30 *Human Identity*

Science has told us nearly everything about man except his identity. The psychologist has analysed our minds and discovered much about them. Medical men have probed into our bodies and found how they work. The anthropologist has shown how we have developed and the sociologist has revealed the effects of living with other people. We don't lack information about ourselves. But who are we? What are we for? These questions can never be answered by science. Where can we find an answer? To find it one must go to someone far wiser and greater than ourselves who is nevertheless like our human selves. Christ, the greatest man who has ever lived, provides the answer. We will discover who we really are if we look to him.

May

1 *Action and Contemplation*

In all of us there is a mixture of a person of action and a person of contemplation. There are times when we want to do things and other times when we want to withdraw within ourselves. There is within us a constant tension between being an individual and being part of a greater whole. Hence there are times when we love to be on our own knowing that our integrity depends upon just being ourselves. And there are other times when we are thankful to belong to the social structure around us. We are creatures of opposites. Just as electricity has two poles, so do human beings and we have to struggle to resolve them. We are made up of a great number of conflicting emotions and to find peace we must go outside ourselves. St John says of Christ: 'He knew what was in man.' Christ understands the tensions which afflict man and tells him: 'My peace I give you, not as the world gives do I give it to you.'

2 *Easter*

Most glorious Lord of life, that on this day
Didst make thy triumph over death and sin;
And having harrowed hell didst bring away
Captivity thence captive, us to win:
This joyous day, dear Lord, with joy begin,
And grant that we for whom thou didst die
Being with thy dear blood clean washed from sin,
May live for ever in felicity.
And that thy love we weighing worthily,
May likewise love thee for the same again;

And for thy sake that all like dear didst buy,
With love may one another entertain.
So let us love, dear love, like as we ought,
Love is the lesson which the Lord us taught.

EDMUND SPENSER 1552–1599

3 *On being Umble*

How little you know of the rightful umbleness of a person in my station, Master Copperfield. Father and me was both brought up at a foundation school for boys; and mother she was likewise brought up at a public sort of charitable institution. They taught us a deal of umbleness; we was to be umble to this person and umble to that; and to pull off our caps here, and to make bows there; and always to know our place and abase ourselves before our betters. Father got the monitor medal for being umble, so did I. Father got made a sexton by being umble. 'Be umble, Uriah', says Father to me, 'and you'll get on.' It was what was always being dinned into you and me at school; it's what goes down best. 'Be umble', says father, 'and you'll do.' And really it ain't done bad ... I'm very umble to the present moment, Master Copperfield, but I've got a little power.

David Copperfield CHARLES DICKENS 1812–1870

4 *The Value of Faith*

Very often I am asked about what people like to call my philosophy of life. When it is put that way it always seems to me to be rather a formidable expression and one too profound to respond to in simple terms. All the same, like everyone else I am sure, I do have certain principles and values which have always loomed large in my approach to life and the problems we all face in living it to the best of our abilities. Now as I approach my 84th year, it seems even older when I see it in print, I find it interesting to reflect on what has made my life, even with its moments of pain, such an essentially happy one. I have come to the conclusion that the most important element in human life is faith. If God were to take away all His blessings, health, physical fitness, wealth, intelligence and leave me but one gift, I would ask for faith – for with faith in Him, in His goodness, mercy, love for me and belief in everlasting life, I believe I could still be happy, trustful, leaving all to His inscrutable providence.

Time to Remember ROSE KENNEDY

5 *Final Examination*

Two small boys saw their grandmother reading her prayer book. One of the boys said to the other: 'What's grandma doing?' The other replied: 'She's swotting for her finals.'

The whole of our lives is a swotting for our finals. Then we shall have our final examination. We will not be judged by how clever we have been. Our pass marks will be based on the kind of way we have lived; on the kind of person we have been. We have to keep on swotting for this because we don't know when the chief examiner, Christ, will be present. We must prepare for it by prayer and good works. The Gospels give us all kinds of good advice of how we should conduct ourselves and give us confidence that we will have very good marks when our exam takes place.

6 *Gandhi*

An excellent example of Christ's words 'that if anyone strikes you on the right cheek, turn to him also the other' was Gandhi. He read those words in the Bible and they set him on the course of non-violence. He was, to look at, a most unlikely revolutionary who initiated an extraordinary liberation movement. Someone has written: '... that wisened seventy-seven-year-old man had done more to topple the British Empire than any man alive.' Whether those words are true or not what is true is that Gandhi's doctrine of non-violence mobilised the masses of India; that with his spirit of poverty he drew countless numbers to himself.

Christ's words however do not mean that every Christian must be a pacifist. There are occasions when violence is justified to protect one's home or children for example. Aggression is wrong; self-protection may not be. But there are many occasions when love rather than force is more powerful in overcoming enmity.

7 *The Devil*

The mediaeval world had no illusions about the devil. It did indeed represent him as a figure of fun, a thing of horns and hooves and a tail, but this was to show that in spite of his superior intelligence he was the biggest 'damned' fool in creation since he exchanged eternal happiness for a moment's pride. At other times he was portrayed as a more flamboyant Mephistophelean figure making pacts with mortals for their souls. But here again it was realised that he was only a character in a legend embodying a truth that a man who sins grievously is handing himself over to the devil's power for a few minutes satisfaction. Many people laugh today at the idea of the devil's existence but no one can deny that there are evil forces in the world waging against those of the good.

8 *Self-deception*

Thackeray said of Pendennis: 'Having a lively imagination he mistook himself for a person of importance very easily.'

All of us deceive ourselves in some way or other because none of us know ourselves perfectly. We may think we are a certain type of person when in reality we are someone quite different. But though self-deception is a universal failing it is by no means always pride that blocks self-vision; a sense of inferiority can do the same. To rid oneself of self-deception is a very arduous process. So many of our most powerful 'drives' lie in the unconscious. Their influence upon us is profound and they are not discovered by any illumination of thought. Some of these influences are seen, like icebergs, just above the surface but most lie well below and thus we do not know the full depth of our being. Here humility is required. We need to turn to God: 'He knows our frame; he knows that we are but dust.'

9 *Misunderstanding*

The advance of science and technology has not only brought the world closer together geographically, but has also increased tremendously the flow of ideas. The aeroplane and the internal combustion engine have made travel swift and easy; the telephone, television, radio and newspapers have brought the minds of people into close contact with one another. All kinds of obstacles, which in the past stood in the way of easy communications, have been swept aside. But in spite of all this there is one form of communication which still presents formidable difficulty, and which science can do little to overcome. That is the personal contacts which involve insight and understanding of another person's character and personality. 'We are like islands', wrote Kipling, 'and we shout at each other across a sea of misunderstandings.' It is our duty to try and understand people. If we pass wrong judgements upon others we are passing such judgement upon ourselves.

10 *Work*

Cardinal Cardjin wrote: 'It is work that must continue God's act of creation, make use of creation, discover all the riches within creation and place them at the disposal of humanity in order that it may attain its destiny. Without work there is nothing, neither moral, intellectual or religious.'

Work, if properly directed is an act of worship of God. It is man's way of praising, reverencing and serving Him. God has designed all human beings to be workers. The whole mechanism of their make-up makes this clear and He has also imparted a solidarity to the human race with its accompanying obligation of mutual help. Those who enrich themselves by their efforts have the right to the fruit of that effort but their work should not be wholly dedicated to self but should also be for the benefit of others.

11 *Magnanimity*

Magnanimity soars up to Heaven and looks down on all dominion of fortune with pity and disdain. Its aims and designs are transcendent to all concerns of this little world. Its objects and its ends are worthy of a soul that is like God in Nature; and nothing less than the kingdom of God, his life and image; nothing beneath the friendship and communion with him can be its satisfaction. The terrors, allurements and censures of men are the dust of its feet; their avarice and ambition are but feebleness before it. Their riches and contentions and interests and honours but insignificant and empty trifles. All the world is but a little bubble; infinity and eternity the only great and sovereign things, wherewith it converseth. A magnanimous soul is always awake. The whole globe of the earth is but a nutshell in comparison of its enjoyment. The sun is its lamp, the sea its fishpond, the stars its jewels, men, angels, its attendants, and God alone its sovereign delight and supreme complacency.

THOMAS TRAHERNE *c.* 1637–1674

12 *The Great Plague*

Nursery rhymes have a history behind them and sometimes not a pleasant one. Children sing the following verse little realising its sinister past.

Ring a ring of roses
A pocketful of posies
Atishoo! Atishoo!
We all fall down.

The verse refers to the great plague that struck England more than 300 years ago. It was caused by fleas carried on rats. The plague killed one-fifth of London's population. The words of the rhyme refer to the rosy marks on the chests of the plague victims, the nosegays that people carried thinking they would prevent infection, the convulsive sneezing and then the fall down in death. Prayers are still said every year in one Midland village for those of the villagers who died in the plague.

13 *The Prayer of Faith*

The only way we can get in touch with God is through prayer. And prayer requires great faith and a confidence that with God's help all will be well in the end. The pilot of an aircraft flying at night keeps on course as long as he is in touch with the control tower by radar. He can pilot the aircraft through darkness without seeing his way ahead and bring it safely to its destination. In the same way a person of faith makes his way through darkness and difficulties by using the radar of prayer to keep him in touch with his control tower, God. There may well be times when he feels he is going off course and cannot see what lies ahead. Like the pilot he must do some blind flying. Yet as long as his faith is strong he knows he can travel forward and arrive safely at his desired destination.

14 *Covenant of Love*

The whole of Scripture is the story of God's communicating love. God spoke out of the darkness of history to His people binding them to Himself in a covenant of love and in its pages He expresses His love in language that is both beautiful and endearing. Perhaps the most expressive metaphor of love in the Old Testament is that of the bride and bridegroom. Through the mouth of the prophet Ezechiel God speaks of a marriage between Himself and His people and His sorrow when the marriage breaks down because of their infidelity. 'When I passed you and looked upon you, behold you were at the age for love . . . I plighted my troth to you, and entered into a covenant of love with you . . . and you became mine!'

This shared covenant of love grew closer as history developed until finally it broke down completely the partition which had come between God and His people by the coming of His Son.

15 *Violin-maker*

George Eliot put the following words into the mouth of the great violin maker Stradivari:

> If my hand slacked
> I should rob God since He is fullest good
> Leaving a blank instead of violins.
> I say not God Himself can make man's best
> Without best man to help Him.

The poet brings out the fact that God cannot do our work without us. If Stradivari refused to make violins God could not make them. He could make far better violins but they would not be the ones that Stradivari refused to make. We need God's cooperation to do anything, but if we refuse to do something which it is our duty to do, then we are 'leaving a blank' because we are refusing God's gift of divine help and willing cooperation.

16 Life's more than Breath

Life's more than breath and the quick round of blood,
'Tis a great spirit and a busy heart;
The coward and the small in soul scarce do live.
One generous feeling, one great thought, one deed
Of good, ere night, would make life longer seem
Than if each year might number a thousand days
Spent as is this by nations of mankind.
We live in deeds, not years; in thoughts, not breaths;
In feelings, not in figures on a dial.
We should count time by heart-throbs. He most lives
Who thinks most, feels the noblest, acts the best.

Festus PHILIP JAMES BAILEY 1816–1902

17 Last Words

The dying words of great men and women do not always reflect their life's work and aspirations; but very often they do, and there is a certain fascination about them especially when they are spoken by great Christians. 'Death, my sister, welcome be thou' clearly comes from the heart of St Francis. It is interesting to compare the dying words of two Thomases. Wolsey said: 'If I had served my God as I have served my king he would not have given me over in my grey hairs.' Thomas More said: 'I die the king's servant but God's first.'

Modern times shed an interesting sidelight on the characters of two English cardinals. Cardinal Manning said: 'I am glad to be able to do everything in due order. I have laid aside the yoke, my work is accomplished.' Cardinal Wiseman on being asked how he felt replied: 'I feel like a schoolboy going home for his holidays.'

18 *Father into Thy Hands*

'Father, into Thy hands I commend my spirit' were the dying words of the greatest man who ever lived. His death was terrible yet He met it as every Christian should with great peace and acceptance of the will of God.

No wonder so many Christians have used those words before they died. Bishop Fisher of Rochester, Lady Jane Grey, Mary Queen of Scots, Christopher Columbus, Pope Pius X to name just a few. All saw life in the light of eternity and knew that death was but a gateway to a glorious future. Perhaps their spirit can be summed up in that of some Christians who had been condemned by communists to be shot at 5.00 p.m. When they heard that the sentence had been postponed till 5.30 p.m. they grumbled that they had been deprived of half-an-hour of eternity.

19 *Sermons*

From the beginning of time preachers have been the subject of many quips and reproaches. Such remarks as 'a preacher is one who talks in another person's sleep' are typical of many. This latter proved true in that mighty orator St Paul. We read in the Acts of the Apostles that he talked so long that a young man fell out of a window asleep and was killed. Sermons can be very dull; they can be full of wind and monotony; they can be quite incomprehensible. But granted that some sermons are dull, ill-prepared and tediously long, it is also true that bad reception is more often the ultimate and principal cause of boredom. One should at least go and be prepared to listen, remembering why the priest is in the pulpit. He is fulfilling a command of Christ: 'Go into the whole world and preach the Gospel to every creature.'

20 *What's in a Name?*

Most of us deeply resent our good name being called in question. If anyone attacks it our shackles tend to rise and we return insults with good measure. The Puritans protected their names by giving them good religious prefixes. This was in the days of 'Praise-God Barebone'. There is a jury list compiled in those days which shows each member had adopted a pious first name; among them 'Stand-fast-on-high Stringer', 'Fight-the-good-fight of faith White', 'More-fruit Flowler' and 'Kill-sin Pimple'.

There is nothing wrong in desiring to defend one's good name but one must not be too pernickety about it. 'What's in a name?' asked Shakespeare and answered: 'That which we call a rose by any other name, would smell as sweet.' We should not be over sensitive about our label. What is much more important is what we are in ourselves.

21 *Justice*

In this God's world, with its wild-whirling eddies and mad foam-oceans, where men and nations perish as if without law, and judgement for an unjust thing is sternly delayed, dost thou think that there is therefore no justice? It is what the fool hath said in his heart. It is what the wise, in all times, were wise because they denied, and knew forever not to be. I tell thee again, there is nothing else but justice. One strong thing I find here below: the just thing, the true thing. My friend, if thou hadst all the artillery of Woolwich trundling at thy back in support of an unjust thing; and in-finite bonfires visibly waiting ahead of thee, to blaze cen-turies long for thy victory on behalf of it – I would advise thee to call halt, to fling down thy baton, and say 'In God's name, No!' Thy success? Poor wretch, what will thy suc-cess amount to? If the thing is unjust, thou hast not suc-ceeded; no not though bonfires blazed from North to South, and bells rang, and editors wrote leading articles, and the just thing lay trampled out of sight, to all mortal eyes an abolished and annihilated thing. Success? In few years thou wilt be dead and dark – all cold, eyeless, dead; no blaze of bonfires, ding-dong of bells or leading articles visible or audible to thee again at all for ever: what kind of success is that?

THOMAS CARLYLE 1795–1881

22 *Prudence*

Two boys were standing by a ditch of considerable width at the bottom of which was a morass. One of the boys when challenged to jump it refused saying: 'I'm not a fool; I'm not going to risk fouling my clothes.' The other boy made the jump and arrived safely on the other bank. The first boy could be praised for his prudence and the second for his courage in willing to take risks. No doubt the world is better because there have existed dare-devils; people we might say are lacking in prudence yet now and again achieve greatness. Prudence in the natural order may sometimes be disregarded for a greater good but it may never in the supernatural order. No risks can be taken in the spiritual life – no foolish leaps which may land one in a moral morass. Supernatural prudence guides the intellect towards the supreme truth and the will towards the supreme good.

23 *Destiny*

There have been those who say that we are driven along the road to an inevitable destiny like characters in some Greek tragedy caught up in a web of circumstances from which it is impossible to escape. Theology has not escaped such sentiments. Some forms of Christianity have fatalistic doctrines according to which man is at the mercy of divine decrees, his fate predetermined by them. What is forgotten is that God governs his creatures according to their nature. He has given men freedom of choice and it is in accordance with that freedom that His providence over them operates. A Russian novelist wrote: 'People are people and not the keys of a piano.' We are not so played on by God that we are forced to produce a particular tune. It is a pessimistic philosophy which says of life:

Tis a cheque-board of Nights and Days
Where Destiny with Men for Pieces plays.

24 *Captains of the Soul*

We are dependent upon the world in many ways. We need the air and the soil. Biological factors, hereditary ones, initial endowments of physique, intelligence, temperament play upon us having an inevitable influence but they do not force us to act in a particular way. Neither the world or God is our ultimate determinant. Always we remain 'Masters of our Fate and Captains of our soul'. But though this is true we cannot thwart God's overall plan for the world. It is woven according to a pattern and though individual threads may be broken, always in the end the full design will appear. Part of the mystery of God's providence is that we do not know how it works and the part we play in it, even when our sins seem so opposed to it.

25 *Providence*

Robert Browning wrote:

Our times are in his hand
Who said 'A whole I planned'.

We cannot see the whole of God's plan. We can only see the bits and pieces like jig-saw ends lying scattered in the box. We are too close to earth to see how the pieces fit together. We have to wait until the consummation of things before we see the blue-prints unrolled and the full pattern revealed. What we do know now is that everything has a purpose, has its part to play in the scheme and thus God's wisdom shines out of the tiniest microcosm as it does out of great world events. We cannot know how the divine wisdom works; why, for example, there seems to be so much disorder in the world such as earthquakes, floods, cruelty amongst men towards one another. What we do know is that out of evil God draws good. He is not mocked and evil cannot destroy His plan.

26 *Looking Back*

In the Old Testament we get glimpses of God's plan for the world. We read how He spoke to Abraham, to Moses and to others. Those words revealed His plan. His call to Abraham to leave his pagan home and to found a new race in a strange land was the way He set His plan in motion. All His dealings with Moses from the rescue of his people from Egyptian captivity to the making of the Covenant and the journey to the promised land were all part of His design. His subsequent care of the people He had chosen, in spite of all their infidelities, was the furthering of it. He even, as Scripture tells us, made use of a pagan king, Cyrus: 'For the sake of my servant Jacob and Israel, my chosen, I call you by your name, I surname you, though you do not know me.' God made use of him to free His chosen people from the bondage of Babylon so that they could make their way back to the land in which the Saviour of the world would live and die.

27 *Freedom and Providence*

The relationship between freedom and God's providence
has racked the brains of theologians, and brought the knives
out, but since no answer is possible it is far better to be a
realist and concentrate on the facts rather than the problem.
And this brings us to the question of how we should react to
this providence of God in our personal lives. We know that
God 'foresees all our steps'. 'His eyes are on the ways of
men.' We can, like St Paul: 'Kick against the goad' or, as he
did in the end, submit ourselves to the will of God. God has
given us freedom and He wants us to use it in co-operation
with His will.

'Uncle Joe,' said someone to an old man who was always
cheerful in spite of having had more than his share of life's
troubles, 'how have you managed to remain so cheerful and
calm?'

'Well, I will tell you', replied Joe: 'I'se jus' learned to
cooperate wid the inevitable.' This is what we should do as
Christians seeing in the inevitable God at work in our lives.

28 *Living Faith*

We all need faith, a real living faith in the power and love of
God who has 'all things in His hands'. This faith is essential
so that we can understand what is good for us and for the
world. 'If only I had God's omnipotence,' cried a preacher
'how I would change the world.' Then he paused for a
moment and added: 'But if I had His wisdom also I would
leave everything as it is.'

What a mess we would make of things if we had the world

at our disposal for twenty-four hours to change it in accordance with our ideas. Our attempts to create a worldly paradise would certainly end in disaster. The ancient prayer gives the correct answer: 'God grant me the courage to change the things I can change, the serenity to accept the things I cannot change, and the wisdom to know the difference.' We cannot answer all the riddles of creation:

> Deep in unfathomable mines
> Of never-failing skill,
> He treasures up His bright designs
> And works His sovereign will.

29 *Hammer Blows*

When Benjamin Disraeli was once asked how he kept on without seeing results he replied: 'Have you ever watched a stonecutter at work? He will hammer away at a rock perhaps a hundred times without a crack showing in it. Then at the hundred and one blow, it will split in two. It is not alone that blow which accomplished the result but the hundred others before it as well.'

So it is with many things in life. We wish to solve some difficult intellectual problem; we must hammer away at it, giving it mental blows. At first we see no results and then comes the final effort when it opens out and reveals itself. We wish to play an instrument. One placing of one's fingers on it will produce nothing. We must do it again and again until our purpose is fulfilled. We wish to gain some request from God. We must storm Heaven; hammer away in prayer and then, as Christ said: 'He who perseveres to the end will be saved.'

30 *The Universal Christ*

I see His blood upon the rose
And in the stars the glory of His eyes,
His body gleams amid eternal snows,
His tears fall from the skies.

I see His face in every flower;
The thunder and the singing of the birds
Are but His voice – and carven by His power
Rocks are His written words.

All pathways by His feet are worn,
His strong heart stirs the ever-beating sea,
His crown of thorns is twined with every thorn,
His cross is every tree.

JOSEPH PLUNKETT 1887–1916

31 *The Spirit and Flesh*

Robert Bridges, in his preface to *The Spirit of Man*, wrote:
'Man is a spiritual being and the proper work of his mind is
to interpret the world according to his higher nature and to
conquer the material aspects of the world so as to bring
them into subjection to the spirit.' St John puts it more suc-
cinctly: 'Only the Spirit gives life; the flesh avails nothing.'

There are many indications in modern life to show that
these words are often ignored. The squalor in big cities, the
ever growing rat-race for greater wealth side-by-side with
the increase of poverty, the prostitution of beauty in many
forms, are just a few. The ignoring of the spirit in man is

the refusal to accept the divine in him. Father Zossima in *The Brothers Karamazov* said: 'A great deal on earth is hidden from us, but there is given to us in recompense the secret conviction of our living link with another world, a heavenly and loftier world; and the very roots of our thoughts and sensations are not here but there, in other worlds.'

June

1 *Holiness*

The trouble about words is that so often one uses them in one sense and people think of them in another. This is particularly true of words with a religious connotation such as holiness. Holiness is often thought of against a background of stained-glass windows and haloes and pious attitudes. The word at times becomes in peoples' minds a synonym for sanctimoniousness. Most people would dislike being called holy, not from humility, but because of the implication that they were in some way inhuman. This of course is nonsense. The word holy has an Anglo-Saxon origin. Literally it means perfect, healthy, whole. A person cannot be wholly a person without holiness; without it he cannot be spiritually healthy. 'This is the will of God your sanctification', said St Paul. It is the duty of every human being to respond to God's will.

2 *Daily Life*

The world has many quite normal holy people. They are not angelic disembodied spirits. They are not bathed in celestial light or perfumed with odours of sanctity. They go about their ordinary everyday affairs, bringing up their families as best they may and carrying out their duties to their fellow men. They are completely unselfish and ever ready to help those in need. They have no visions and work no miracles. They wear hats not haloes. They are not canonised for their splendid lives. They are men and women who love God and their neighbour and prove it in a thousand different ways in their work, their prayer and acts of self-sacrificing charity. Holiness makes real people and not sham angels. God created people for holiness and therefore it is in the power of all to achieve it. It does not demand extraordinary feats of courage but only the carrying out of God's will in the circumstances of daily life.

3 *Creative Love*

Human life without love is empty and profitless. A loveless person is narrow, pinched, unproductive of good:

> The wind blows out of the gates of day
> The wind blows over the lonely heart
> And the lonely heart is withered away.

Love is the most powerful creative force in the world. It is love that moves the great artists of the world to express themselves in masterpieces of painting, music and poetry. Love has been the spur to great enterprises of the mind and adventures into the unknown. Love of knowledge has driven men to search into the secrets of matter and to reach out to the moon and planets. And it is love that makes the world go round. The whole maturity and well-being of a person depends upon love. That we can love is God's great gift to us.

4 *Love and Sex*

The word love today is often identified with the word sex. The realities are clearly not the same. Sex finds its fulfilment in love. To attempt to realise sexual desires without love results in nothing but frustration. Many worship at the shrine of sex for its excitements and pleasure but so often the god turns out to be false and the only return they get from him is disillusionment and weariness. Sex without love is like a drug without healing power. It is separating the animal from the spirit in a person and so making him less human. Only when sex and love are allied is the truth about sex revealed and its dignity and beauty known. Those who love one another lose their lives to one another and find them again in one another. Their children are the fruits of love's creative power.

5 *The Spirit of Love*

All true love, whatever form it takes, love of knowledge, love of art, love of adventure, love in marriage is the breath of the Holy Spirit upon the earth. The Spirit is personified love, the consummation of the union of Father and Son. His creative breath gave birth to the world and thus the world was conceived in love. All human beings are in some way under the power of the Spirit; even those who refuse to recognise Him cannot evade Him, for without Him they are nothing. This is true of natural love but for this to reach its perfection it must be transfigured not only by the creative power of the Spirit but by His sanctifying presence. Christ, under the inspiration of the Spirit, brought redemption to all true human love making it creative of eternity by placing in it a divine spark. The love of Christ and human love become in this way identified.

6 *The Power of Love*

All love, whether it be strongly emotional, as in marriage, or less so in other forms, powerfully affects the personality. Love completes and refines the personality, raising it to new heights and revealing what is deep and eternal in its being. It awakens within the personality great qualities that have lain dormant. It liberates from pettiness by creating generosity of spirit. It gives and takes (for both elements must be present in love) and results in both self-surrender and possession of what is good. All this is seen to a supreme degree where love is greatest. Hence that great lover, St Paul, could cry out: 'Neither death, nor life, nor angels, nor principalities, nor power, nor things present, nor things to come, nor any other creature, shall be able to separate us from the love of God'. Few of us perhaps can repeat those words with complete sincerity but we can approach to the ideal in our daily gropings to purify our love; a love expressed in our work, in our prayer and in our relationship with our fellow human beings.

7 *Union*

The Vicar of Wakefield declared: 'I chose my wife as she chose her wedding gown for qualities that would wear well.' This does not mean that love will not have to struggle to give full expression to itself. There can be quarrels between lovers, many upsets, darkness and hurts, but if the love is true and Christ-like, it will, like Christ Himself, rise to new life. Love will 'wear well' if it is based on the divine. The Spirit of Christ will be its binding force. And just as love in marriage manifests itself most perfectly in union, so does all love in any person who is searching after God, whether that person be a mystic or one who simply feels drawn to God. There is always the desire to get into touch with Him and so become in some way united to Him. These people also go through periods of trouble and darkness but the power of the Spirit of Love within them creates strength and peace making their love durable.

8 *Goodness*

Oh, yet we trust that somehow good
Will be the final goal of all,
To pangs of nature, sins of will,
Defects of doubt, and taints of blood;

That nothing walks with aimless feet;
That not one life shall be destroyed,
Or cast as rubbish to the void,
When God has made the pile complete.

That not a worm is cloven in vain;
That not a moth with vain desire
Is shrivelled in a fruitless fire,
Or but subserves another's gain.

Behold, we know not anything;
I can but trust that good shall fall
At last – far off – at least, to all,
And every Winter change to Spring.
ALFRED LORD TENNYSON 1809–1892

9 *The Space Age*

We are living in the dawn of a great space age when astronomy and technology are continually opening out new vistas in the sky. Men have stood on the moon and no doubt will one day stand on Mars. And the more that space is conquered the more insignificant in size the planet on which we live and die becomes. And, because of this, there are those who say that this cannot be a God-made planet on which the incarnation took place. Is God interested in so diminutive a structure? After all it is only a tiny grain in the immensity of limitless space.

The mistake here is evaluating the worth of something by its size and not by its intrinsic importance. An astronomer was lecturing on the Milky Way and speaking of the enormous size of the stars which go to make it up, showing how tiny our world is in comparison. One of the audience said: 'If our world is so tiny compared with the other heavenly bodies, how can God take an interest in us tiny midgets clinging to it?' The astronomer replied: 'That depends upon how big a God you believe in.'

10 *Christian Unity*

St John in his epistle says: 'This is the message we have heard from Him and proclaim to you that God is light and in Him there is no darkness at all.'

Christ is that light and he is ready to shine on all men to reveal the truth about Himself. Opposed to this light is darkness, the darkness of ignorance and bigotry and sometimes hatred.

The blackness of the night in which Christ died was symbolic of the satanic darkness that was trying to extinguish the light. At Easter the light conquered the darkness, bursting from it with splendour amid the sunrise of the Resurrection. This was a time of complete renewal; it was the vindication of truth and love. And it is here, surely, in the life, death and resurrection of Christ that not only hatreds and ignorance and bigotry should be dispelled (and today, thank God, much of this has happened) but the unity of Christendom should be achieved. Christ longed for this unity and prayed for it before He died.

11 *God's Wonderful Works*

'Sing a new song to the Lord for he has worked wonders', sang the psalmist. The magnificence of God's works should inspire us with a sense of wonder. There are a million things for us to wonder at. Carlyle wrote: 'Indeed it is well said, in every object there is inexhaustible meaning; the eye sees in it what the eye brings means of seeing.'

In other words there is nothing that cannot be a source of wonder. The tiniest object is full of mystery. God has made us in such a way that we cannot know anything in Nature completely. There is always an element that eludes us and so provides a source of wonder. And the greatest source of wonder should be that all things are God's handiwork. The psalmist crys out: 'O Lord, what a thing to be wondered at is your name over the whole earth. I look up at the heavens, the work of your hands, at the moon and stars which you have set in their places.' There is so much to wonder at in the universe, its intricacy of design, its unity of purpose, and above all the indwelling presence of the divine artist.

12 *Two Windows*

There are two windows, the view from which give two very different views of life. The first window is in the play by Samuel Beckett, *Endgame*. One of the characters says: 'I once knew a madman who thought the end of the world had come. I used to go and see him in the asylum. I'd take him by the hand and drag him to the window. Look, there. All that rising corn. And there. Look. The sails of the herring fleet. All that loveliness. He'd snatch away his hand and go back into his corner. Appalled. All he had seen was ashes.'

The other window is a real one. It is in a little church in Southern Ireland. All the windows in the church, except this one, are of stained glass representing Christ and His saints. This one window is of plain glass and through it may be seen a breath-taking view; a lake studded with green islets and backed by range after range of purple hills. Under the window is an inscription: 'The heavens proclaim the glory of God and the firmament shows forth the work of His hands.'

The two windows remind one of the verse:

Two men looked through prison bars
One saw mud, the other stars.

13 *God's Presence*

When we say that God is present everywhere we mean that He knows everything, keeps everything in being, and in some mysterious way is present in everything without actually being identified with it. St Paul told the Athenians, amid derisive laughter, that: 'In him we live and move and have our being'! The poet tells us:

> Earth's crammed with Heaven
> And every common bush afire with God
> But only he who sees takes off his shoes,
> The rest sit round and pluck blackberries.

Those who have true vision to see the presence of God are like Moses who approached the burning bush with reverence and, taking off his shoes, because he was standing on holy ground, heard the voice of God. All ground is holy to those who have the vision of faith since it is the tabernacle of the presence of God.

14 *To God the Father*

> Great God; within whose simple essence we
> nothing but that which is Thyself can find;
> when on Thyself thou didst reflect they mind,
> Thy thought was God, which took the form of Thee:
> And when this God thus born, Thou lov'st and He
> lov'd Thee again, with passion of like kind,
> as lovers' sighs which meet become one mind,
> both breath'd one Spirit of equal deity.
> Eternal Father, whence these two do come
> and wil'st the title of my father have,
> an heavenly knowledge in my mind engrave,
> That it Thy Son's true image may become:
> incense my heart with signs of holy love
> that it the temple of thy Spirit may prove

HENRY CONSTABLE 1562–1613

15 *The Glory of God*

When Moses came down from the mountain after communing with God the people were so dazzled by the reflected glory in his countenance that they were unable to look at him. 'Show me your face', said Moses to God. And God replied: 'No man can look upon my face and live.'

Moses was bathed in the reflected light of the glory of God but he was unable to gaze upon the glory itself. God dwells in inaccessible light. But what was not given to the chosen people of God of old was given to the new chosen people with whom Christ walked and talked in Palestine.

'The same God who bade light shine in darkness has kindled a light in our hearts whose shining is to make known His glory as He has revealed it in the features of Jesus Christ. For Christ is the glory of God. The glory of his people Israel.' Thus wrote St Luke. And St John tells us that His miracles were 'signs of His glory'. And Christ said: 'He who sees me sees the Father also.'

16 *Sharing in God's Glory*

Christ is the image of the Father, the splendour of His substance, the brightness of eternal light. It is true that the outward manifestation of that glory was hidden during His life. 'He emptied Himself of His glory.' Yet at the same time St John could boast: 'We saw His glory, the glory as it were of the only-begotten of the Father, full of grace and truth.' This is the splendour of the incarnation; that God's glory appeared among us in human form and that this glory was to be shared with us. This was Christ's prayer at the last supper. He prayed for the outward restoration of His own glory: 'That glory which was His before the world was with Him.' Then He went on to say: 'And the glory thou has given to me I have given to them.' Christianity is the sharing of the glory of God. A Christian soul is illuminated by that glory; it burns like an incandescent flame within him.

17 *Suffering and Glory*

St Paul tells the Romans: 'I reckon that the sufferings of this time are not worthy to be compared with the glory to come, that shall be revealed in us.'

This contrast which St Paul makes between the tribulations of this life and the joy to come, helps to solve the problem of pain which has puzzled so many human minds, though clearly it does not give a complete answer. Most people surely would willingly accept a month of great pain if, in exchange, they could be certain of perfect happiness for the rest of their lives. What is a month, they would say, compared with a lifetime of bliss? St Paul is echoing those sentiments.

What are fifty, sixty or seventy years of a certain amount of suffering compared with an eternity of glory? How insignificant are this world's tribulations compared with the joy to come. If only, in other words, we could realise what the joy of being with God for ever means how willingly we would accept the pains and trials of this life to gain it.

18 *Why Pain?*

People ask: why have pain in this world? Couldn't the good God give us eternity without it? There is no completely satisfying answer to this because it is a mystery within a mystery, the mystery of love. Love and pain are inextricably joined together in this life; they form part of our humanity. Christ, who was perfect love, cast aside His glory, entered into our world of pain and died upon a cross. His pain was the fruit of love. 'Greater love no man has than to lay down his life for his friend.' There is a deep joy in suffering for somebody one loves. Even the sinless Mary suffered. Her suffering rose directly from her love. Indeed the more she loved the more she suffered. So love has placed us in this world because love wants love.

19 *The Light of the Spirit*

Without the light of the sun and moon our world would be a dead and barren place. There could be no physical growth without it, no beauty of design. There would be no civilisation and culture as we know it. And what is true of physical light is also true in its own way of the light of the Spirit. Without it the world is sterile without beauty of soul or harmony. St Basil wrote: 'The lightning-strokes of divine beauty are beyond utterance; no speech represents them, no hearing receives them. You may talk of the brightness of the day-star, the moon's shining, the light of the sun; all are nothing in comparison with that glory, and fall far short of the true light than does the deep gloom of a moonless night of the clearest noonday.'

This beauty is invisible to bodily eyes, perceived by soul and mind alone, if perhaps it shone upon any of the saints and left them with an intolerable sting of desire! In our modern world it may be difficult to realise the beauty and splendour of the light of the Spirit but this does not detract from its reality.

20 *The Journey*

The journey from darkness to light is a constant theme of ancient folk-tales and sagas. It represents the longing of humanity for a more perfect and happier existence. It is the journey from ignorance towards the truth, from trials and tribulations towards peace. In the Grimm tale of the king's daughter in her search for the prince, we are told that she climbed one evening into a tree to spend the night there. When midnight drew near she saw in the distance a small light and thought: 'Ah, now I shall be saved.' This hope of salvation in some form is common to mankind. The human caravan travelling across the world is always making for the light but so often the light proves to be a mirage because it is sought in the wrong places. Yet, always hope remains:

For there is good news yet to hear and fine things to be
  seen
Before we go to Paradise by way of Kensal Green.

21 *Aspiring Minds*

Nature, that fram'd us of four elements
Warring within our breasts for regiment,
Doth teach us all to have aspiring minds;
Our souls, whose faculties can comprehend
The wondrous architecture of the world,
And measure every wandering planet's course,
Still climbing after knowledge infinite,
And always moving as the restless spheres,
Will us to wear ourselves, and never rest,
Until we reach the ripest fruit of all,
That perfect bliss and sole felicity,
The sweet fruition of an earthly crown.
Tamburlaine CHRISTOPHER MARLOWE 1564–1593

22 *Hope*

The supernatural virtue of hope is the complete trust that God will lead us to the eternal heights and will provide the means of arriving there, if we do what He requires of us. We do not rely simply on our own powers. We realise that we are helpless on our own. We need the co-operation of God. Hence in our upward journey there is a partnership between ourselves and God. It is not possible to have the virtue of hope unless this is realised. If we think we can climb the heights alone we become guilty of presumption; if, on the other hand, we think we can remain inactive and that God will carry us along we again become guilty of the same vice. There was hope in the apostle's voice when he said: 'I can do all things in Him who strengthens me.' St

Paul told Titus 'to live soberly, justly and godly in this world, looking for the blessed hope and coming of the great God and Saviour Jesus Christ.'

Right through Scripture there is an encouraging note of hope, but with the warning that it can be lost through slackness. 'He that thinks himself to stand let him take heed lest he fall', wrote St Paul.

23 *The Bible and Forgiveness*

The Bible is a history of forgiveness. It begins with a promise and culminates with a cross. The promise is carried forward in the story of Israel. Without God's constant forgiveness not even a remnant of Israel would have survived to usher in a new order of things in which the most sublime act of forgiveness took place. Faithlessness, fickleness, downright ingratitude were overlooked again and again. Sins 'red as scarlet' were pardoned so that new starts were made, new hope inspired, new ground won and, what was more astonishing, sin so vile and evil became a 'happy fault' through the advent of Christ.

Thus was God's mercy towards His people vindicated and His prophecy about them through Isaiah fulfilled: 'You have burdened me with your sins, you have wearied me with your iniquities. I am He who blots out your transgressions for my own sake and I will not remember your sins.'

24 *Christ and Forgiveness*

Christ was the embodiment of forgiveness. He was generous towards failures and weaknesses and ever ready to be merciful towards what was most hateful in men. He inspired hope in those who could expect nothing but retribution enabling them to start the battle of life afresh with all their wounds healed. He was always ready to forgive. The only exception being those who refused to forgive. In the parable of the unforgiving servant the latter was thrown into prison and the lesson from his action given universal application by Christ. 'So also my heavenly father will do to everyone of you if you do not forgive your brother from your heart.' Thus Christ made forgiveness an obligation. No one could be His follower unless he had a forgiving nature. And forgiveness was not to be restricted to friends with whom a person might quarrel, enemies also had to be its recipient.

25 *The New Man*

'Brethren, be ye renewed in the spirit of your mind, and put on the new man, who according to God is created in justice and holiness of truth.' So wrote St Paul to the Ephesians.

What is this new man? It is not a superficial transformation; it is radical. Somehow, though remaining the same person, we are to become quite different. The new man sees the world with new vision. He hears what no ordinary ears can hear. He has a wisdom and understanding and insight beyond the power of a normal human brain. Also, he has a life which does not commence with his human birth nor will end with his death. Baptism, the birth of the new man; from that moment he begins to grow with a life that is given to him by Christ. It is this life which enables him to see with the vision that follows from faith. He can hear the voice of God and have 'that mind in him which was also in Christ Jesus'. Outwardly he is the same as any other human being but inwardly he is transformed; new strength and power and an inward splendour beyond imagination is his because now, in some marvellous way, he shares the divine nature.

26 *The World Struggle*

Scripture often represents the great battle that goes on between the forces of good and evil in the form of light and darkness. This is symbolised by the darkness that spread over Egypt during one of the plagues: 'There came horrible darkness in all the land of Egypt for three days. No man saw his brother, nor moved himself out of the place where he was.' But in Israel there was light. 'Wheresoever the children of Israel dwelt there was light.'

From the very start of creation this opposition between the two forces was clear, commencing with the victory of evil over the world, plunging it into the darkness of sin. But God who is light would not allow the darkness to remain and so, in the course of time, he sent forth his light in the person of his Son so that the brightness of eternal light might shine among men. 'The light shines in the darkness, and the darkness has not overcome it', wrote St John.

27 *Wolves in Sheeps Clothing*

Many destructive forces have an insidiously innocent outward appearance. The Trojans of old were warned to beware of the Greeks bringing their gifts, especially the gift of a wooden horse, a loaded gift indeed, full of armed men ready to destroy their city. Christ warned his disciples about this kind of thing: 'Beware of false prophets who come to you in the clothing of sheep, but inwardly they are ravening wolves.'

One cannot judge holiness by outward appearances. It has nothing to do with good looks or a perfect hair-style. A pleasant manner, an infectious smile can be the cloak of evil-doing. The devil can transform himself into an angel of light. We need wisdom to see what is wrong or even evil in certain ideas and sentiments even though they are wrapped in attractive language. The real test of a man's worth is not his outward appearance but his heart set on God and the things of God.

28 *The Reality of Faith*

There are those who say that the man of faith is no more than a child staring into the dark and seeing ghosts; that faith is an illusion, a form of self-deception to give a feeling of security. But the child does not see the ghost however much his fears may cause him to think he does. The man of faith does see the truth amid the darkness standing out sharp and clear. This clarity of vision can no more be explained to the sceptic than light and colours can be described to a blind man. Faith is an illumination of the mind which gives a certainty that cannot be expressed in logic but which is far removed from self-deception. It has its source in Christ of whom Zacharia said that He came 'to give light to those who sit in darkness and in the shadow of death'. Christ is the guarantee of our faith. We see in Him one who is beyond deception, one in whom sincerity and power are the proof that His words are true. The more we get to know Christ through prayer the deeper will our faith be.

29 *The Mystery of Love*

God's presence in an individual is a mystery because it is the mystery of love. It is the love of Father, Son and Holy Spirit. This love gives dignity and greatness to a human being. Man is surrounded by immensities of space and power, star upon star, fiery galaxies, whirling through unimaginable distances and within the confines of matter such explosive forces as to make his strength in comparison infinitesimal. Yet he has a power within him that can reach beyond the furthest stars, that is more powerful than anything the whole world of matter contains:

> For love's the gift which God has given
> To man alone beneath the heaven.

Love is the most powerful force in existence. It is love which unites Father, Son and Holy Spirit and which humanity shares.

30 *Christian Joy*

Christianity is the religion of joy. The Gospels are tidings of great joy. This note of joy rings like a bell throughout the Gospel story. When Christ was born the angel announced to the shepherds: 'I bring you word of a great joy which belongs to all the people.' This great joy was Christ. He brought a new joy into our world. An optimism which the world had not known before was created by Him. He himself was a man of joy. He radiated happiness wherever He went, healing men's bodies and souls. He was joyful in His friends and in His work. His joy corresponded to that universal law that the happiest people in the world are those who do most for others. Fundamentally His joy arose from His relationship with His Father. He delighted in doing always the things that pleased Him. This should be the source of our joy too. Our happiness depends upon our right relationship with Him. We cannot as Christians be pessimists. We always have a bright future.

July

1 *Sorrow and Joy*

Even in the most discouraging moments in the New Testament a great note of joy is sounded. When the apostles with the Master gather together for their last meal Christ speaks of joy. One would have thought that the shadow of the coming terrible events would have reduced them to feelings of sorrow and foreboding. Instead Christ encourages them and says: 'These things I have spoken to you that my joy may be in you and your joy may be full.' When He sees they are troubled He says: 'Let not your hearts be troubled, believe in God, believe also in me.' And He added: 'My joy I give you and your joy no man takes from you.'

After His departure at the Ascension when one would expect the disciples to be sad at His going, we are told that they returned to Jerusalem with great joy. This was because they had the commission to be witnesses of Him. When they were flogged for their faith the disciples depart from the Council rejoicing 'that they are counted worthy to suffer dishonour for His name'. Paul, in his Roman prison facing death, dictates: 'Rejoice, Brethren, again I say rejoice.'

2 *The Greatest Love*

Sometimes people ask the question why did Christ die on a cross? Was it necessary to save men from their sins? It certainly was not necessary. He need not have died at all. We could have been saved in many ways. God could, for example, simply have willed our salvation. Why didn't he?

Here we come up against the sublime mystery of love. Love is the key to the whole work of redemption. And love is the reason why suffering and death were involved. Christ said: 'Greater love no man has than to lay down his life for his friend.' Suffering and dying for others is indeed the supreme sacrifice of love and since God so loved the world he decided to win the world back to Himself through the suffering and death of His Son. Love died on the cross so that love might be reborn in men. And the very amount of suffering this involved was purely and simply the overflowing of love.

3 *Superabundant Love*

In Marlowe's play, *Faustus*, when the devil comes for the soul of Faustus he cries out:

> See, see how Christ's blood streams in the firmament;
> One drop would save my soul, half a drop, Ah, my
>   Christ

It was not one drop that was spilt; it was every single drop. Thus God's love was superabundant. Like human love, the divine delights in union, in the sharing of life. So God made man and became a member of the human community and gave Himself completely to it in life and death. He took His place at its head, becoming its representative so that He could, in its name, make restitution for wrongs committed. All of us hung on the cross with Christ and all of us died with Him so that we could rise with Him to new life. In this way perfect reparation was made to God; the complete restoration of the balance of justice was brought about. We can only gaze with amazement at this immense love that went to such length on our behalf.

4 *Tears over Jerusalem*

The Gospel tells us: 'When Jesus drew near to Jerusalem, seeing the city, He wept over it saying, if thou hadst known and that iñ this thy day, the things that are to thy peace; but now they are hidden from thy eyes.'

Some forty years after Christ was crucified, women and children would die amid dreadful carnage and the city and temple would be reduced to rubble. Allied to His sorrow for them was one arising from patriotic love. Christ was a Jew and every Jew loved Jerusalem which was the centre of their religious life and the epitome of their culture. Nor was it simply the ruin of the splendid temple and the ancient city that He wept for, but the faithlessness of many of its people. For hundreds of years there had been a special relationship between these people and their God. And now when He had come to them in human form as their Messiah and king, their leaders had rejected Him and refused to recognise Him. The tears of Christ are one more proof that He was like us in all except sin:

> Tears and smiles like us he knew
> And he feeleth for our sadness
> And he shareth in our gladness.

5 *Astrology*

St Augustine in his *Confessions* relates that his friend Ferminius, like himself, came to see the absurdity of astrology. Ferminius gives his reasons: 'My father told me that, when my mother was expecting my birth, a female slave of his friend was also pregnant, and this was of course known to her master who used to register with the greatest care even the birth of his puppies. But while they were counting with laborious accuracy the days, hours and minutes, the one for his wife, the other for his slave, it happened that both women were delivered at the same time, so that they were forced to make the same horoscope, down to the smallest particulars, for the son and the baby slave ... Neither could mark the least difference in the position of the stars. And yet I was born in a good position, advanced rapidly along the bright paths of the world, grew in wealth, rose in rank; while the slave, as I was told by one who knew him, remained what he was, without any freedom from his slavery.'

6 The Vine

'I am the true vine', said Christ. This vine did not spring up suddenly. It had roots in the past. There was a very long period of fertilisation of the soil before the vine appeared. God's providence was at work bringing together the necessary elements for its growth. If one reads the Old Testament with spiritual insight, one can see how God prepared the ground so that the vine could grow and send forth branches and fruit. God wanted the grace-giving power of the vine to be given to all men. From the beginning, God had Christ in mind to be a power and a strength to all mankind. He created men and women to become a world-wide chosen people united to Christ as branches are united to a vine. Thus the vine was not to remain static in growth. Through the ages it was to develop, sending forth more and more branches until its full height and maturity had been reached.

7 *The Eagle and the Wren*

Once long ago the birds gathered in a wood and agreed that the one who flew highest would be their king. Naturally the golden eagle was certain that he would win. There was no doubt in his mind that he would go higher than any other bird. The tiny wren challenged the eagle. Up flew the mighty bird of prey, going up and up until he was out of sight. But the little wren had secretly perched on the eagle's back and, being quite fresh, flew even higher. That is how the little wren became the king of birds. That little fable illustrates what Christ said – that His followers should not attempt to lord it over another, or to try and compete with one another in greatness. They must learn the lesson of humility, then, like the little wren, they will rise to great heights. It is the humble who will be exhalted. People who, like the golden eagle, boast of their prowess, often become so full of themselves that there is no room for God.

8 *The Sparrow and the Swallow*

The beautiful eighty-third psalm pictures the sparrow and the swallow building their nests close to the temple precints, furnishing an image of the peace and security to be found in the house of the Lord. It is to the Lord's house that the faithful come to find peace of soul. They come from their work in factory, field, office or home, like homing birds, to the dwelling place of God, to receive help and protection and renewal of spirit. And when they leave the material building, they know that their hearts have become the dwelling-place of God. His grace has enriched them through that indwelling presence. In this way they are drawn away from the dark valleys of materialism and tepidity into the warm light of Him who illuminated the world. Always in life we should have this sense of the protective power of God. The birds in the psalm nestle near God's house but we, by God's love, become living temples of the Holy Spirit.

9 *A Modern Good Samaritan*

A certain Mr Minton wrote a book in which he described a terrible thing which happened to him at a railway station. He was drinking a cup of tea when he went suddenly completely blind. When it happened he reached out to somebody standing near and asked him for help. The man said he would and left but never returned. After a time Minton clutched someone else. Again, he explained what had happened to him and again was promised help, but help never came. In all he asked seven people for help, all said they would and went away leaving him alone in his darkness. The eighth person promised help and went and got it. Minton tried to thank him but his benefactor would have none of it. 'Good heavens', he said, 'that's nothing – anyone would have done the same.' Whom do you think was neighbour to the blind man?

10 *Credulity*

Father Ronald Knox in his book *Enthusiasm* tells of a woman, Jemima Wilkinson, who asserted that she had died and come back from the grave as a reincarnation of Christ. She started a new religion and obtained a few devotees. One day she said she would walk on water, would they like to see it? Her followers naturally replied that they would. So they all went down to a pond and before she stepped out she turned to them and said: 'Do you really believe I can do this?' They all rapturously replied: 'Yes we do.' 'If you believe it,' she said, 'there's no point in my doing it.' It is surprising how credulous some people can be. They will accept the most astonishing events on the flimsiest of evidence. Many people are superstitious, believing all kinds of things or events will either harm them or bring them benefits. For such people the supernatural is often a fantasy.

11 *Life*

Christ illumined the chaos and darkness of humanity by revealing its potentialities and uniting His life to it in abundance. He expressed in His own person the way to live. He was no pessimist nor an out-of-the-way visionary. He was very human. He loved to be with simple people. He enjoyed beautiful scenery, human relationships and children, all that goes up to make the human story. At the same time He saw everything in terms of the eternal and expressed its ultimate meaning in very beautiful and telling language which has captivated posterity ever since.

The Christian recognises this and it helps him to escape

from the mechanisation of society. Christ constantly spoke of life and it is this word life that is the key to the perplexities of existence. In Him who said 'I am the Life' resides the answer to the question 'What is life for?' Christ is the centre of human life. He gives it scope and elevates it above its natural level and awakens in it aspirations for the infinite. His words are life.

12 *Divine Vision*

Christ loved beautiful things but His mind did not rest on their surface. He used what is passing and temporal as expression of the eternal. His parables, His allusions to nature, His metaphors and similes were attempts to disclose to our blind eyes the unseen kingdom of God. He held up many things before us, things that would in a few days or weeks fall to dust and told us to see the eternal in them. He ransacked the world for examples, marking off common and familiar things as mirrors of what is everlasting. So light, wine, vines, water, shepherds, sheep, goats, trees and many others things became transformed with a light from another world. Worldliness has been defined as looking at things which are seen but only closely enough to see their market value. The divine vision of Christ saw deep into things and saw the indwelling presence of the everlasting God.

13 *Words of Life*

The words of Christ are like no other words which are usually the means of expressing thought and communicating ideas. His words are loaded. They contain power. They communicate not only ideas, but strength and spiritual energy. They are hammer-strokes breaking down barriers of pessimism and despair. They open out the way to men's highest hopes and aspirations. They are a continual challenge so that men have never been able to disengage themselves from their impact. They are words full of grace. If one listens to them with real devotion their grace is received. They promise life; not human life but a divine which reaches beyond all human affairs to God himself. The words are full of promise. Like a searchlight they illumine human actions and minds revealing their purpose and worth. St John tells us: 'Of his fullness we have all received grace upon grace.'

14 *Reconciled to Death*

Since Nature's work be good, and death doth serve
As Nature's work: why should we fear to die?
Since fear is vain, but when it may preserve:
Why should we fear that which we cannot fly?

Fear is more pain than is the pain it fears,
Disarming human minds of native might:
While each conceit an ugly figure bears,
Which were not evil well view'd in reason's light.

Our owly eyes which dimm'd with passions be,
And scarce discern the dawn of coming day,
Let them be clear'd and now begin to see,
Our life is but a step in dusty way.

Then let us hold the bliss of peaceful mind,
Since this we feel, great loss we cannot find.

SIR PHILIP SIDNEY 1554–1586

15 *Union with the Risen Christ*

The Christ who rose from the darkness of the tomb to new life rose with a body that had been battered and beaten to death so that humanity who rose with Him could be united with Him in a new body made up of His followers. In this new body the experience of life and death was to start anew. This new body, like the body of Christ, was to be wounded and mocked. Its journey through the world was to be a way of the cross. It was to suffer countless crucifixions and each time to rise again, strengthened by suffering and persecutions. At times it would be left in ruins but the wasteland created would become a clearing-ground for a greater and finer edifice. And just as the enemies of Christ, who had Him put to death, were the instruments by which He conquered death, so the attacks upon His followers give new life to their cause.

16 *The Suicide of Self*

The process of life and death experienced by Christ should also be the lot of each individual Christian. Christ said that a man must lose his life in order to gain it. In other words the suicide of self must be the preliminary to a new life for it is only from the tomb of self that resurrection with Christ can take place. Egocentricity is the death of Christ in a person since it is the death of love. Where there is no true love there is no Christ.

The ugly sisters flaunt their finery at the ball, but it is Cinderella who is transformed and who wears the wedding garment and is loved by the prince. Men, like Christ, must make their humble way of the cross to their resurrection. Their love for Christ should be the panacea of their pain and united with Him they receive the guarantee of eternal life. St Paul told the Romans: 'If the Spirit of Him who raised Christ Jesus from the dead dwells in you, He who raised Christ from the dead will give life to your mortal bodies also, through His Spirit who dwells in you.'

17 *Light before Men*

When Mother Teresa was in Australia she came across an old man in Melbourne, living in squalid quarters. She insisted on cleaning his room for him. In the room was a beautiful lamp covered with the dust of years. She said to him: 'Why don't you light your lamp?' Then she added: 'Will you light your lamp if the sisters come to see you?' A few days later he sent her a message: 'Tell my friend, the light she has lit in my life is still burning.'

Christ said: 'So let your light shine before men that they will see your good works.' This was what Mother Teresa did. The dirt covering the beautiful lamp was a symbol of men's neglect of the old man; the cleaned and lighted lamp was a sign of great charity and love. Christ was the light of the world; his light shone in Mother Teresa and so the light she shed was the reflected light in her of Christ.

18 *The Armour of Light*

In modern times one hardly expects to see a knight in shining armour except on stage or screen. He stands for a byegone age of chivalry; he conjures up pictures of jousting and rescuing fair maidens from terrible predicaments. He fought evil always in its various forms. We are urged by St Paul: 'Put on the armour of light to ward off the works of darkness.' Hence we are to protect ourselves against evil by armour, but not armour made of any earthly material but one made by light. What is this light? It is the spirit of Christ who said 'I am the light'. We are to clothe ourselves with this light of Christ – to 'put on Christ'. Through Him and in Him we will overcome the darkness of evil. 'For our wrestling is not against flesh and blood, but against principalities and powers, against the rulers of the world of darkness, against the spirit of wickedness in high places,' said St Paul.

19 *The Vineyard*

The parable that Christ gave about the vineyard may seem at first sight full of injustices. Surely the employer, people may say, was acting unjustly in paying the same wages to those who had only worked for an hour as to those who had worked all day. One can imagine the rumpus and the strikes that would follow if a modern employer acted like that. But the parable illustrates very vividly the difference between God's standards and human ones. It came as a shock to those who had borne the heat and burden of the day in the vineyard to discover that their pay was exactly the same as that of those who had only worked for an hour in the cool of the evening. It is true they had received what they had contracted for but they felt injured. But surely it is very fortunate that in the Lord's vineyard all are not paid according to their deserts. If the Lord never gave what is superabundant we should be in a sorry plight. Suppose He only rewarded those who lived good lives and never gave grace to sinners on their death-bed it would go hard with us all.

20 *Irritants*

We are all inclined to feel tired and impatient at times. Life suddenly goes all wrong. The fire won't light, we spill tea over the best table-cloth, and to crown all, a sneeze suggests a coming cold. Little things, strange to say, are far more annoying and irritating than big things. There are few of us who cannot stand up to real tragedy when it comes; there are few who cannot find resignation when big griefs shadow the heart. But little things can warp and break – if they are allowed to do so.

The only way to break the thrall of little things is to learn to laugh at them. This is not easy, but it can be done. If one fumes and frets and worries, one's nerves will get frayed and, after a little while life will hardly be worth living. But, if one laughs, things do not seem half as bad and the sting is taken out of trifles that might otherwise prove fatal. Laughter is a good tonic. It is good to make use of it to counteract the little annoyances and jolts of daily life.

21 *Introspection*

A thoughtful person looking in upon himself, must surely feel in his being some power which does not come from himself, which could not come from himself, some power which is not human but comes ultimately from God. A person's very existence seems to demand it. This perception is, of course, reinforced by faith. But even without faith there are intimations of the infinite within his finite being. The stage manager in Thornton Wilder's play, *Our Town*, leans against the procenium and says: 'We all know that something is eternal. And it ain't houses and it ain't names and it ain't even the stars – everybody knows in their bones that something is eternal and that something is to do with human beings ... There's something way deep down that's eternal about every human being.'

God planted the seeds of eternity in man when He 'breathed into his nostrils the breath of life'.

22 *The Two Worlds in Man*

Newman wrote in his *Dream of Gerontius*:

O man, strange composite of heaven and earth,
Majesty dwarfed to baseness, fragrant flower
Running to poisonous seed, and seeming worth
Cloaking corruption.

We belong to two worlds, the material and the spiritual; the secular and the religious. Our danger lies in trying to live in one of these worlds to the exclusion of the other. Our task is to harmonise the two. The secular and the spiritual must be combined. There should not be a division between religion and life. The former gives depth and value and purpose to the latter. We all need bread but we cannot live by bread alone.

23 *The Bridge*

The novel *The Bridge of San Luis Rey* is an example of how what seemed a terrible catastrophe was from another point of view a blessing. A number of people plunged to their death when the bridge collapsed. Those who saw what had happened blamed God saying He was cruel to allow such a thing to happen. But an examination of the lives of those who had died showed that God had chosen the right time for each to depart. They had all had enough of life. In each case death was simply the crowning of an existence which had reached its fulfilment. We only see one side of life's coin; there is another known only to God. Like those below the bridge we can cry out that God is cruel or, if we have faith that:

God moves in a mysterious way
His wonders to perform.

24 *Everyman*

In the old morality play *Everyman* there are characters like Wealth, Pleasure, Power, Good Deeds and, the principal one, a universal person called Everyman.

The play expresses a truth about death for in it Death steals from Everyman everything to which he clings. Wealth goes, so does Power, Pleasure, Youth and Beauty. But Death cannot steal Everyman's soul. Nor can it take his Good Deeds. They will go with him to the land which lies ahead. Life is a journey and, as the play indicates, at the end of it we must cast off most of our luggage when we reach the final crossing. In fact the only luggage we can take with us is, as Ronald Knox has pointed out, charity. Good Deeds are useless without it as St Paul has told us.

25 *Ceaseless Creation*

It is as true to say that I was created as to say I am being created. I am the object of ceaseless creation. Just as a song only lasts as long as the singer sings, so I only exist as long as God not only wills me to exist but also keeps me in existence by His power. God cannot leave me alone. This is surely a source of wonder. I cannot raise my arm, cannot speak or walk or breathe without God's co-operation. God and I walk hand in hand. And what is true of me is true of all the world, even of those who turn their backs on God. Even with them God co-operates with their freedom.

The only quality God cannot co-operate with is sin. Sin belongs to humanity alone. And since sin is evil and evil is a deprivation of the good, it is humanity's cry – 'I will not serve'.

26 *Wonder and Awe*

The philosopher Kant said: 'Two things fill my mind with ever renewed wonder and awe the more often and the deeper I dwell on them; the starry vault above me and the moral law within me.'

Wonder and awe are the offsprings of mystery. There is mystery in the existence of the moral law within human beings and there is mystery in the vast space studded with stars. Neither of them are self-explanatory. They have inspired many people to accept the existence of a supreme being who is responsible for them and who Himself is a mystery. Abraham Lincoln is only one of them. He said: 'I never behold the stars that I do not feel that I am looking in the face of God. I can see how it might be possible for a man to look down on earth and be an atheist, but I cannot conceive how he could look up into the heavens and say there is no God.' The psalmist expressed it well when he said: 'The heavens proclaim the glory of God.'

27 *West Side Story*

In that fine musical *West Side Story*, the young hooligans had gathered in the drug store and were boasting of their crimes. At length the old man who ran the drug store cannot stand their talk any longer and he shouts out in fury: 'You make this world lousy.' And one of the young gangsters replies: 'We found it that way.'

No doubt his words were true. They were the product of slum conditions, of broken homes, of criminal surroundings. These things were contributors to their characters but were not the whole story. They still had the freedom to break away. God, when he made our world, saw that it was good. It is human beings who so often make it 'lousy'. They are the destructive forces in society. Christ said that evil came from the heart of man and not from external circumstances.

28 *The Human Will*

Willpower is the driving force in a human being. It is under the direction of the mind which points the way to go. Unfortunately, because a human being's mind is defective in many ways, it can and does direct the will at times in the wrong direction. Sometimes it freezes the will, as Augustine found when he said: 'I sighed, chained as I was, not by iron, but by my own will stronger than iron.' Fortunately he broke the chain and found deliverance.

The human will has the extraordinary power of turning in against itself and gaining victory over itself. It can be trained and tamed, or it can run wild and cause havoc becoming the source of misery when it could be that of happiness. Christ taught us to pray to His Father, 'Thy will be done'. If we tune our will in accordance with that of God we can be sure that it is being directed in the right direction.

29 *The Gift of Existence*

There are those who say: 'I did not ask to be born; why should I have to live against my will?' This is practically a form of blasphemy. It is the desecration of the divine image in man and hence the rejection of God Himself. Existence with all its possibilities of greatness is God's great gift. It is true that a person cannot climb the heights without toil and self-sacrifice. He must give all to obtain all, to destroy self to develop it. Only out of the grave of self can the true self emerge. This is what Christ said: 'A man must lose his life to gain it.' On the ruins of egoism will joy and acceptance of life flourish. When a person craves only after the finite in himself, existence becomes meaningless and suffering hateful. It is when he strips himself of his sensuous and selfish desires that life's significance and immortal purpose becomes clear.

30 *The Sobbing Sahara*

The Arabs have a wonderful legend about the sobbing of the Sahara. When, on a quiet starry night, a soft breeze passes over the immense desert and makes myriads of small grains of sand clash, it produces the effect of a painful moan emitted by a mortally wounded gigantic wild beast. 'Can you hear it?' says the caravan guide. 'The desert is weeping. It complains of having been transformed into an arid desert; it cries out for the flowery gardens, the waving fields of corn, the beautiful fruit with which it was once loaded before it burnt up and became a desert.'

A person can sometimes become a desert of loneliness, a bleak and arid existence, a turmoil of frustrated desires. So it was with Hamlet: 'It goes so heavily with my disposition that this goodly frame the earth, seems to me a sterile promonitory.' Love must be the fertilising agent to make joy and hope flourish; a love of God and a love for men.

3**1** *The Cry of Anguish*

The cry of man's anguish went up to God,
Lord, take away my pain
The shadow that darkens the world Thou hast made;
The close coiling chain
That strangles the heart: the burden that weighs
On the wings that would soar –
Lord, take away pain from the world Thou hast made
That it love Thee the more.

Then answered the Lord to the cry of the world,
Shall I take away pain,
And with it the power of the soul to endure,
Made strong by the strain?
Shall I take away pity that knits heart to heart,
And sacrifice high?
Will ye lose all your heroes that lift from the fire
White brows to the sky?

Shall I take away love that redeems with a price,
And smiles with its loss?
Can ye spare from your lives that would cling unto mine
The Christ on His cross?

ANON

August

1 *The Month named after Caesar*

August has received its name from Caesar Augustus, the first and greatest of the Roman emperors. It was said of him that he found Rome made of brick and left it made of marble. During his reign the Temple of Janus was closed, signifying that the Roman world was at peace. This had happened only twice in the whole history of the Republic. Tremendous events took place during the rule of this great emperor which had a world-wide impact but he never knew the greatest of them all. How could he have known of the birth of a child named Jesus in a small province whose mother came from an obscure village? Yet that child was to turn 'marble' Rome into the greatest kingdom the world would ever see. Instead of the pagan temples, great Christian churches would arise. Instead of the ancient pagan gods, the true God would be worshipped in a way that Rome had never known. From that child would come a moral and spiritual force that was to be revolutionary in human affairs, upsetting values and standards and creating entirely new ones.

2 *The Apples*

Benjamin Franklin once illustrated to a young mother who was leading a small child by the hand how possessions can bring unhappiness. He took an apple from a basket and gave it to the child who clutched it with joy. Then he offered another apple and the child joyfully grasped hold of it in his other hand. Then Franklin proffered a third apple. The child tried to hold on to the three apples but dropped them all and burst into tears. 'See,' said the philosopher to the mother, 'here is a little man who has too much wealth to enjoy it. He was happy with two apples but unhappy with three.' This is a reminder of Robert Louis Stevenson's words:

> The world is full of a number of things.
> I'm sure we should all be as happy as kings.

So we should if we are not too grasping.

3 *Problems of the Universe*

Goethe wrote: 'Man is born not to solve the problems of the universe, but to find out where the problem begins, and then to restrain himself within the limits of the comprehensible.'

The universe is full of puzzles; many of them unsolvable. But this should not prevent our studying them and trying to find out why they are puzzles and remain complete mysteries. The trouble is that we do not always know the limits of the comprehensible. History has shown that on many occasions people have thought they have reached the limits only to find that they have merely broken through. It is in the world of the supernatural that the biggest puzzles exist and it is there that we should restrain ourselves within the limits of the comprehensible. An obvious example is the puzzle about suffering and evil in the world. Many have tried to solve it but no one has managed to do it completely. We have to leave the answer, in the end, to God.

4 *Appearances*

The celebrated criminologist, Lambroso, once made an experiment. He collected together a large selection of photographs of bishops, divines, statesmen, philosophers and philanthropists. He then mixed them up with those of murderers, sadists, crooks and burglars. Having shuffled them well, he asked a number of experienced judges, doctors, psychologists and policemen to pick out the criminals. All failed. The number of the well-behaved characters selected was as great as that of the evil-doers. Evil is within a person and not in his features. Christ said of some of the Pharisees that they were like whited sepulchres, beautiful on the outside but inside full of corruption. The devil can clothe himself as an angel of light.

5 *Legend of the Angel*

Abou Ben Adhem (may his tribe increase)
Awoke one night from a deep dream of peace,
And saw, within the moonlight in his room,
Making it rich, and like a lily in bloom,
An angel writing in a book of gold:—
Exceeding peace had made Ben Adhem bold,
And to the presence in the room he said:
'What writest thou?' The vision raised its head,
And with a look made of all sweet accord,
Answered, 'The names of those who love the Lord.'
'And is mine one?' said Abou. 'Nay, not so',
Replied the angel. Abou spoke more low
But cheerily still; and said 'I pray thee then

Write me as one that loves his fellow men.'
The angel wrote, and vanish'd. The nest night
It came again with a great wakening light,
And show'd the names whom love of God had blest,
And Lo! Ben Adhem's name led all the rest.

LEIGH HUNT 1784–1859

6 *Night and Day*

There is an old story about the Rabbi who asked his disciples how they knew that night was ended and the day was on its way back. 'Could it be', asked one, 'when you can see an animal in the distance and tell whether it is a sheep or a dog?' 'No', the Rabbi replied. 'Could it be', asked another, 'when you can look at a tree in the distance and tell whether it is a fig or an olive tree?' 'No', said the Rabbi. 'Well, what is it then?' asked the disciples. 'It is when you look on the face of any man or woman and see that he or she is your brother or sister. Because if you cannot see this, no matter what time it is, it is still night.' St John expressed this when he said: 'He who says he is in the light and hates his brother is in the darkness still.'

7 *Old English Saying*

Take time to work – it is the price of success
Take time to think – it is the source of power
Take time to play – it is the secret of youth
Take time to be friendly – it is the road to happiness

Take time to read – it is the foundation of wisdom
Take time to dream – it is hitching your waggon to a star
Take time to love and be loved – it is the privilege of the
    gods
Take time to look around – it is too short a day to be
    selfish
Take time to laugh – it is the music of the soul.

8 *The Christ Presence*

At the end of two years spent in prayer by myself and others for this end, namely that Our Lord would either lead me by another way, or show the truth of this – for now the messages of Our Lord were extremely frequent – this happened to me. I was in prayer one day – it was the feast of the glorious St Peter – when I saw Christ close to me, or to speak more correctly, felt Him; for I saw nothing with the eyes of the body, nothing with the eyes of the soul. He seemed to me to be close beside me; and I saw too, as I believe, that it was He who was speaking to me. As I was utterly ignorant that such a vision was possible, I was extremely afraid at first, and did nothing but weep; however, when He spoke to me but one word to reassure me, I recovered myself, and was, as usual, calm and comforted, without any fear whatever. Jesus Christ seemed to me to be by my side continually, and as the vision was not imaginary, I saw no form; but I had a most distinct feeling that He was always on my right side, a witness of all I did; and never at any time, if I was slightly recollected, or not to much distracted, could I be ignorant of His near presence.

ST TERESA OF AVILA 1515–1582

9 *Two Sisters*

Robert Louis Stevenson tells the story of the two sisters who inhabited a single room in Edinburgh. They quarrelled over some theological controversy and fell out so bitterly that they never spoke to one another again. Whether from lack of means or the Scottish fear of scandal they continued to stay where they were. A chalk line drawn upon the floor separated their two domains. It bisected the doorway and the fireplace, so that each could go out and in and do their cooking without violating the territory of the other. So for years they existed, in a hateful silence; their meals, their ablutions, their visitors exposed to an unfriendly scrutiny. They were two sisters rivalling in unsisterliness. Well we might say with Puck: 'Lord, what fools these mortals be.' If only one of them could have brought herself to say three magic words, 'I am sorry', this hateful existence might well have ended.

10 *Dust and Glory*

Scripture tells us that we are but dust, but that God took hold of the dust, breathed His spirit into it and transformed and transfigured it so that it acts with an energy far beyond its own capabilities. The works of this 'quintessence of dust' become shot through with the grace of God, and though Heaven is hidden from our eyes by a material curtain, yet Heaven and earth are intermingled with our affairs so that everything we touch and see has Heaven in and about it. Thus our life becomes an adventure of the spirit. Through the dimness of earth we struggle to the dawn of Heaven.

Our instruments of work, typewriters, brooms, computers, business letters, all become conductors of the eternal. Our destiny depends upon our use of them with our minds directed towards the glory of God.

11 *The Praise of God*

'Your praise, O God, like your name, reaches to the ends of the earth', said the psalmist. How is God praised throughout the world? Is He praised in the middle of the Sahara or in the depth of the sea? Is there anywhere where He is not praised? The answer is given by the psalmist. God is praised in all His creatures. Every thing that exists is praising its creator by the very fact of its existence. The birds flying through the air, the fish swimming in the sea, the animals roaming through the forests, the trees and plants growing, the very atoms that make up the material world, are all unconsciously giving glory to their maker. A great song of praise goes up continually from earth to heaven, myriads of different voices yet blended in unison of a single theme. It is man's duty, above all, to give praise to his maker. His song should dominate the song of the world. It is through His mind and heart that all things and living creatures sing their greatest act of praise.

12 *Peace*

> My soul, there is a country
> Far beyond the stars,
> Where stands a winged sentry
> All skilful in the wars,
> There above noise and danger
> Sweet peace sits crowned with smiles,
> And one born in a manger
> Commands the beauteous files,
> He is thy gracious friend,
> And (O! my soul awake!)
> Did in pure love descend
> To die here for thy sake,
> If thou canst get but thither
> There grows the flower of peace,
> The rose that cannot wither,
> Thy fortress and thy ease;
> Leave then thy foolish ranges;
> For none can thee secure,
> But one, who never changes,
> Thy God, thy life, thy cure.

HENRY VAUGHAN 1622–1695

13 *Honourable Work*

After eleven years of hard and prosperous labour, encouraged by constant tributes of admiration, Sir Walter Scott found that the firm which published his books had gone bankrupt. This failure threw on him responsibility for £130,000. He felt the dishonour of bankruptcy and determined to fight against it. During the last six years of his life he laboured to get rid of the huge debt. This had been incurred through no fault of his own. During those six years he worked hard at writing books. His wife died soon after the struggle began but, though feeling sick at heart, he laboured on, writing for honour. He nearly succeeded in clearing the debt and what he failed to do personally the royalties from his books accomplished.

14 *Sloth*

I passed by the field of a sluggard
by the vineyard of a man without sense;
and Lo! It was all overgrown with thorns;
the ground was covered with nettles
and its stone wall was broken down.
Then I saw and considered it;
I looked and received instruction.
A little sleep, a little slumber,
A little folding of the hands to rest,
and poverty will come upon you, like a robber,
and want like an armed man.

Book of Proverbs

15 *Uniqueness*

Every man is an island in the sense that there is something in him which is incommunicable, something unique. People are not mass produced. They do not come off a conveyor-belt like some manufactured product with the same label and contents. Each person is separately blue-printed in the mind of God, not as regards his nature but as regards his identity. All human beings have human nature in common and this enables them to communicate with each other. They all know what it is to love or fear and sympathise. All can say with Shylock: 'If you prick us do we not bleed? If you tickle us do we not laugh? If you poison us do we not die?' A human being's greatness lies in his personality, in the mysterious 'I' that makes him king of his existence, distinct from his fellows, a unique being in history never to be repeated.

16 *Tolerance*

We all live with other people. We are constantly brushing against them. We are not dealing with puppets or creatures of cold logic. They have blood in their veins; they have hearts that beat as well as brains which function. Many of them are bundles of prejudices, are touchy, are motivated by vanity. All of them are beings of emotion just as we are. Our approach to them should be one of tolerance and understanding if we are not to rub against them like flint flashing fire. We must build up in ourselves creative emotions that will enrich and warm our personality and create a corresponding glow of friendship about us. We must, in other words, learn to tolerate difficulties of character and expect others to tolerate them in ourselves.

17 *Religious Blindness*

The father in that excellent book by Edmund Gosse, *Father and Son*, was a very devout man, a lover of the Bible and a man of prayer. At the same time he was very narrow and prejudiced, and he succeeded for a time in forcing his views on his son. Christmas Day was to him a heathen festival and his son relates that 'he would denounce the horrors of Christmas until it almost made me blush to look at a holly-berry'. The father gave orders that there should be no difference in the meals for that day. He was obeyed, but the servants secretly made a small Christmas pudding and gave a slice to the son. Then the son, overcome with remorse, burst into his father's study and cried: 'Oh! Papa. Papa, I have eaten flesh offered to idols.' It took some time amid the sobs to explain what he had done. Then the father sternly said: 'Where is the accursed thing?' He went into the kitchen, seized what remained of the pudding and ran to the dust heap where he flung 'the idolatrous confectionery' into the rubbish.

18 *Sincerity*

In the novel *Two a Penny*, by Stella Linden and David Winter, Jamie Hopkins has visionary illusions of fame and fortune, but lives in an underworld of drugs and criminals. Carol, the girl who loves him and is loved by him, refuses his advances and says she will never marry a sham. Only when he becomes a real person, and that is impossible without the love of God, will she marry him. 'Swinging on the outside is no good if it isn't happening inside,' she said,

'I want my life to be real, Jamie, not make-believe.'
The poet Robert Browning wrote in *Paracelsus*:

Truth is within ourselves, it takes no rise
From outward things, what'er you may believe.
There is an inmost centre in us all
Where truth abides in fullness, and around
Wall upon wall, the gross flesh hems it in,
This perfect, clear perception – which is truth.

19 *The Mice*

There is an old story about a family of mice who lived in a grand piano. They constantly heard the sound of music which they enjoyed though they did not understand it. They paid honour to the great player whom they could not see. One day some of the mice went for a walk. They came back to announce that there was no mystery about the music. It was brought about by wires stretched and vibrated high above the homes of the mice. This discovery caused the mice to disbelieve in the existence of the great player. Then some other mice went on a journey further than the wires and returned to announce the final discovery. It was not the wires but hammers dancing up and down that caused the music. This finally convinced the mice that the great player was only a myth. But the girl went on playing the piano just the same.

20 *Other Mice*

In a letter to Frederick the Great in 1730 Voltaire wrote:
'The mice inhabiting small holes in some immense building
do not know whether that building is eternal, nor who is
the architect, nor why he built it. They try to preserve their
lives, to people their holes, and to escape the preying animals which pursue them. We are the mice, and the Divine
Architect, as far as I know, has not yet told his secret to
any one of us.'

21 *Peace and War*

A man stared up at the great tall United Nations building
in New York and thought about the inscription written
upon it: 'They shall beat their swords into ploughshares
and their spears into pruning-hooks; nation shall not lift up
sword against nation, neither shall they learn war any-
more.' If only, they would, he said to himself.

> Ah love, let us be true
> To one another. For the world, which seems
> To lie before us like a land of dreams,
> So various, so beautiful, so new,
> Hath really neither joy, nor love, nor help for pain;
> And we are here, as on a darkling plain
> Swept with confused alarms of struggle and flight,
> Where ignorant armies clash by night.
> *Dover Bridge* MATTHEW ARNOLD 1822–1888

22 *The Longing for Peace*

All over the world, ordinary people long for peace but no one seems to have the power to bring it about. Science can produce a superficial unity, based on the mass media and easiness of communications. It can help to make people understand that they are involved in each others' lives, whether they wish it or not, and so give them an inkling of the brotherhood of man. But science can only be a tool and not a final cause of unity. The struggle towards world peace cannot be resolved through the achievements of science or on a political level. Disunion springs from the refusal of the Spirit of love in the hearts of men and so unity can only be approached where love is triumphant through the presence of the Spirit.

23 *Facing up to Life*

Outside Rome, in a poor deserted spot, is a little chapel built of grey stone. It is normally empty and set in its ancient stone floor is a plaque giving the reason for the existence of the place. It is the chapel of Quo Vadis. The story goes that it was here that Peter, fleeing from Rome during the persecution of the emperor Nero, had a vision of Christ who asked him the question *quo vadis?* (where are you going?). This question sent Peter back on his tracks to face up to any trials or persecution that might follow. Life for all of us has its ups and downs. We can either face up to them with courage or run away from them. We can, in other words, either play the coward or act as responsible human beings.

24 *The Fullness of God*

The eyes of my soul were opened and I saw the fullness of God in whom I understood the whole world, both here and beyond the sea, and the abyss and ocean and everything. In all these things I saw nothing save the divine power, in a manner indescribable; so that through so much wonder the soul cried with a loud voice saying 'The whole world is full of God!' Therefore I now understood how small a thing is the whole world, that is to say both here and beyond the seas, the abyss, the ocean, and all things and that the power of God exceeds and fills all. Then He said to me: 'I have shown thee something of my power', and I understood that after this I should better understand the rest. He then said 'Behold now my humility'. Then I was given an insight into the deep humility of God towards man. And comprehending that unspeakable power and seeing that deep humility my soul marvelled greatly, and did esteem itself to be nothing at all.

ST ANGELO OF FOLIGNO 1248–1309

25 *Liabilities and Assets*

Whistler, the artist, started out to be a general and was dropped from West Point because he could not pass in chemistry. 'If silicon had been a gas', he said, 'I would have been a major-general.' He might have added that the world would have lost a great artist. Milton's blindness did not prevent his becoming a great poet. What grander symphonies were ever written than Beethoven's and yet he was deaf and towards the end of his life could not even hear his own immortal notes. Nelson never conquered his seasickness. Demosthenes stuttered; he filled his mouth with pebbles and walked along the seashore shouting at the waves until, in spite of his handicap, he became Greece's most famous orator. Defects can become advantages if they are made use of. All of us have reserves of power which we little realise. None of us stretches to full capacity.

26 *Pure Joy*

This is what somebody wrote about George Thomas, a victim of muscular dystrophy: 'Here was a man of keen intellect and most sensitive spirit who in a way asked all of life and in another way nothing. He wanted beauty in all its forms and read the best writers and listened to the best music and kept his spirit eager and alert, for any new experience that might come his way. He was one of the happiest people I have ever met for his interest in everything was intense. He had miraculously kept all his mental and spiritual faculties alive and sensitive to the least vibration of beauty, in fun, sympathy or affection. I don't think there was a moment when he was here that his heart was not full to the brim of pure joy. His poor body was inert and helpless, but all the more it seemed his soul could and did soar.'

27 *Happiness and Pleasure*

Pleasure is not the same thing as happiness. Pleasure is in the nerves; happiness is in the mind and heart. Pleasure feeds on itself and becomes surfeited. If it is made a target it becomes a false friend cheating the one who aims at it. Real pleasure is a by-product of action, the result of doing something well. Happiness on the other hand can be cultivated. The psychologist James said: 'A person is as happy as he makes up his mind to be.'

There are, of course, unhappy moments in a person's life but they should not remain so for long; happiness must be recovered. Happiness shows itself in a deep down peace of spirit. A housewife said: 'I am always happy because I put my religion into my washing.' A life inspired by the love of God is likely to be a happy one; a life led for the sake of pleasure leads to disillusion.

28 *The Nightingale*

Somerset Maugham wrote the fairy tale, *Princess September and the Nightingale.* The nightingale used to come to the princess every day and sing to her. This aroused the jealousy of her sisters who suggested that the bird might fly away. So the princess caught the nightingale and put it in a golden cage. But once the nightingale was caged and unable to be free it could not sing. When the princess said she would take him out every day he replied that he could not sing without freedom. He must enjoy the rice fields and the lake and the willow trees without looking at them through the bars of a cage. 'I cannot sing unless I am free', he said, 'and if I cannot sing I die.' So the princess gave him his liberty.

29 *Recipe for Thoughtfulness*

Take two heaped cups of patience
One heartful of love
Two handfuls of generosity
A dash of laughter
One headful of understanding
Sprinkle generously with kindness
Add plenty of faith and mix well
Spread over a period of lifetime
And serve everyone you meet.

30 *The Death of Sir Walter Raleigh*

Sir Walter Raleigh wrote the following lines on the night before his execution.

Even such is Time, that takes in trust
Our youth, our joys, our all we have,
And pays us but with earth and dust;
Who in the dark and silent grave,
When we have wandered all our ways,
Shuts up the story of our days;
But from this earth, this grave, this dust,
My God shall raise me up, I trust.

When he laid his head on the block he said: 'So the heart be right it is no matter which way the head lies.'

31 *The Present Moment*

The only part of time we can call our own is that split second known as 'now'. We can only live in the present moment; the past is done with and the future lies ahead and we do not know what it contains for us. It is the split second that we live that our fate is decided. 'Now is the acceptable time; now is the day of salvation.' We live and die in the present moment. 'Dost thou love life?' asked Benjamin Franklin; and answered his own question: 'Then do not squander time, for that's the stuff life is made of.'

For those with faith time's end blossoms into eternity
For those with faith time holds hope for the future
For those with faith time is pregnant with eternal power.

September

1 *Love*

So much has been written about love, but much of it is a travesty of the reality being nothing else but sentimentality, sensuality or even lust. True love has a divine element in it. Christ indicated this when He said to His disciples: 'A new commandment I give you, that you love one another as I have loved you.'

Christ is involved in true love. This does not mean that we cannot love without thinking of God and His Christ. It means that if love is true and sincere it is in the poet's words, 'The poured rays of God's eternity'. It is God's infinite love reflected, however feebly, in a human being. Love then is not merely a sentimental feeling. When Christ told His apostles to love one another He meant that they were to put themselves at the service of one another. Love shows itself in deeds rather than in word. It may well involve self-sacrifice and it certainly involves unselfishness.

2 *Christian Duty*

The Christian's duty is to grow in love, to see love at the very centre of creation not only as the origin of all the things that have been made, but also as the power behind all human existence. To realise such love in its fullness is a life-long task. It involves self-forgetfulness and self-giving. One must say 'no' to self at times in order to say 'yes' to God. God sent His Son into the world to show human beings what true love is. St Paul tells us: 'God chose us in Him before the foundation of the world.' Thus human lives are bound up with the life of Christ and therefore they should love one another in Christ. We enter into the life of Christ at the moment when His great act of love, His death, is symbolised and mystically realised in us by baptism.

3 *The Great Fire of London*

Oh the miserable and calamitous spectacle! such as haply the world had not seene the like since the foundation of it, nor to be outdone til the universal conflagration. All the skie was of a fiery aspect, like the top of a burning oven, the light seene above forty miles round about for many nights. God grant my eyes may never behold the like, now seeing above 10,000 houses all in flame; the noise and crackling and thunder of the impetuous flames and ye shrieking of women and children, the hurry of people, the fall of towers, houses, and churches was like an hideous storme and the aire all about so hot and inflam'd that at last one was not able to approach it, so that they were forc'd to stand still and let ye flames burn on, which they did for neere two miles in length and one in breadth. The clouds of smoke were dismall, and reach'd upon computation neere fifty miles in length. Thus I left it this afternoon burning a resemblance of Sodom, or the last day. London was, but is no more.

JOHN EVELYN 3 September 1666

4 *Old Age*

When we for age could neither read or write,
The subject made us able to indite;
The soul, with nobler resolutions decked,
The body stooping, does herself erect.
No mortal parts are requisite to raise
Her that, unbodied, can her Maker praise.

The seas are quiet when the winds give o'er;
So, calm are we when passions are no more!
For then we know how vain it was to boast
Of fleeting things, so certain to be lost.
Clouds of affection from our younger eyes
Conceal that emptiness which age descries.

The soul's dark cottage, battered and decayed,
Lets in new light through chinks that time has made;
Stronger by weakness, wiser men become,
As they draw near to their eternal home.
Leaving the old, both worlds at once they view,
That stand upon the threshold of the new.

EDMUND WALLER 1606–1687

5 *The Beaver*

Sir Osbert Sitwell in his book, *The Scarlet Tree*, tells of a
man who once captured a beaver and decided to make a pet
of it and take it to his country house. To get there he had to
pass through New York and decided to spend a night there
in his flat. His wife received the unexpected visitor kindly

and decided that the best place for the animal to pass the night was in the drawing room in which they placed a box lined with straw to accommodate it. When they entered the room next morning they were confronted with chaos. The animal had escaped from its box and had knocked over a small table on which was a vase of flowers. The water on the floor had brought all the beaver's dam-building instincts into play. It had sawn up all the eighteenth-century chairs and tables and with the aid of cushions and books constructed a remarkable example of a dam.

6 *Temperance*

'Virtue stands in the middle' was a Roman apophthegm. It was an echo of the Greek 'Nothing too much'. The perfect balance must be found in a person's viewpoint if he is truly wise. What makes judgements wrong is generally over-emphasis of some aspects of truth leading to the neglect of another. It is in extremes that error lies. And it is not only in things of the mind that the balance should be kept. An obvious example is food. Over indulgence brings its own woes in the form of indigestion or other stomach troubles. The same is true in regard to drink. A little verse expresses this well:

> God in his goodness sent the grapes
> To cheer both great and small.
> Little fools will drink too much
> And great fools not at all.

There is good down-to-earth wisdom in that.

7 *Aloneness*

Can one ever be completely alone? One can isolate oneself from human company for a while and disengage oneself from the noise and speed of life but can one extricate oneself from them in mind and heart? But even if I can do so – if I could place myself in the completest physical solitude, how much of a solitude would there be within myself, who would bear within myself memories of joy or sorrow, bruises and strains, fears and anxieties, all that goes out from me and comes into me in the mutual reactions of human life and affection? What would be left of myself if I could strip myself of all that has become part of me? Perhaps if I did I would find God, God in myself, myself in God; there would be nothing but God.

8 *The Three-legged Stool*

Parents, teachers and pupils all have their part to play in the work of education. Which of the three is most important? One might just as well ask which leg of a three-legged stool is most important. Take one leg away and the stool will wobble and probably collapse. Parents, teachers and pupils each have their special and unique part to play in education but at the same time theirs is a co-operative effort. Parents give the initial thrust to it. They provide the setting and their task is to continue to take an interest in their childrens' progress. The part of the teacher is obvious. His task is not only to provide knowledge but also discipline of mind and character. The pupils are the last leg of the educational stool. Learning and hard work is their part. The proverb 'you can lead a donkey to the water but you cannot make him drink' can be rendered – neither parent or teacher can force a pupil to drink from the fountain of learning; all they can do is to try and make him thirsty.

9 *The Mine-shaft*

A visitor to Cornwall went for a walk one evening and lost his way. Night came on and he knew that he was close to a number of mine-shafts, many of which had no protecting fences. It was too cold for him to sit and wait for help so he moved cautiously forward but in spite of all his caution he suddenly found himself slipping down a shaft. Fortunately he managed to clutch hold of a protruding piece of rock and hung on shouting for help. It was well over an hour, when exhaustion was about to cause him to let go of his hold, before he was discovered. When this happened and a light was shone down he found that he had been hanging in a filled-in shaft and that terra firma was about a foot beneath him. A good parable of many of our disquieting fears and anxieties.

10 *The Insulated Mind*

There is a higher beauty in the world beyond any that we can see with our human eyes and with which the insulated mind cannot get in touch. The insulating material may take many forms: it may be money or pleasure or sensuality. But the most powerful is pride. Francis Thompson wote:

The angels keep their ancient places.
Turn but a stone, and start a wing.
'tis ye, 'tis your estranged faces,
That miss the many-splendoured thing.

Pervading, penetrating the world is that 'beauty ever ancient, ever new', of whom St Augustine wrote so well. All the splendours of the world are but 'broken lights' of it. We cannot see that beauty unless we ourselves are 'charged' with the grace that makes us alive to it.

11 *Words of Wisdom*

The Book of Wisdom says: 'What folly in man's nature, this ignorance of God. So much seen, and He, who is existent Good, not known. Should they not learn to recognise the Artificer by the contemplation of His works? Instead they have pointed to fire, or wind, or to the nimble air, wheeling stars, or tempestuous waves, or sun and moon, and made gods of them, to rule the world. Perhaps the beauty of such things bewitched them into mistaking it for divinity?'

The vision of the eternal mirrored in the world is only for those whose minds and hearts are not blocked by self-love in its various forms. There is some excuse, as the Book of Wisdom points out, for those whose 'desire is to find God, and in their search they err'. The ones who have no excuse are those who are idolatrous who set up idols of different kinds and in doing so miss 'the many-splendoured thing'.

12 *The Measure of Love*

In the terrible concentration camp of Auschwitz during the Second World War, one of the prisoners escaped and the Nazi commandant, by way of reprisal, ordered ten others to be condemned to death by starvation. Amongst them was a married man with a family; a little Franciscan priest, Father Kolbe, insisted on taking his place.

Kolbe was still alive in the death cell at the end of a fortnight and since the cell was required for somebody else he was finished off with an injection. Love shows itself in deeds rather than words and the measure of love is what a person is willing to give up for it. Christ said: 'Greater love no man has than to lay down his life for his friend.'

13 *Meditation*

Meditation is an excellent psychological tranquilliser. It results in peace of mind and soul and gives a certain depth to the personality. To practice it requires stillness of disposition. It involves a journey into the interior of our being, not in order to concentrate on ourselves, but on the presence of the infinite being of God who alone fully understands us. 'He knows our frame; he knows that we are but dust.' This silence of the spirit is the essential response to the mystery of God. We must be silent in order to listen to His voice. His response is one of union with us. There may not be any corresponding feeling on our part but our good will is the guarantee that it is there. Once we are united with God we can meditate on His presence in creation, in our fellow human beings for there are intimations of Him everywhere.

14 *The Great Mystery*

How can we meditate on God if we don't know who He is?
We cannot have a concept of Him. He is not the superlative
of human qualities. He is a complete mystery in regard to
His essential nature. Yet, though this is true, it is still possible to have indications of His presence. In our meditation
we can raise our hearts and minds to Him through the
creatures He has made. An artist cannot paint a picture
without leaving some stamp of His personality upon it.
God cannot make a world without leaving some impress
of His presence. We can be drawn to Him through His
wonderful works. We cannot know Him as He is with our
minds but we can get to know Him through prayer with our
hearts.

15 *The Inevitability of Death*

In Chaucer's story the merchant of Baghdad sends his servant to the market-place to buy provisions. He came back
white in the face and said: 'Master, lend me your horse so
that I can ride to Samara.' 'Why do you want the horse?'
asked the merchant. 'Because', said his servant, 'when I was
in the market-place I saw Death and he made a gesture
towards me.' 'Very well,' said the merchant, 'you can have
the horse.'

So the servant mounted the horse and rode as fast as he
could to Samara. The merchant then went down to the
market-place and saw Death and asked him why he had
made a gesture towards his servant. 'I did not,' said Death, 'I
was making a gesture of surprise to see him here because I

had an appointment with him in Samara.' If one needs a moral to the tale, it is that it is always better to face up to Death than run away from him.

16 *Adventure*

We cannot all undertake great enterprises or adventurous voyages or perform heroic deeds. Our lives may be very humdrum and we may prefer to be like that. We may be quite content with our round of daily duties and our family life. But there is one adventure we should all embark on which is open to all. This is a spiritual adventure.

Bound up with our physical life is the spiritual. It commences at Baptism and continues until death. It may not seem so glamorous as other kinds of adventure and it may not make a great appeal to the emotions. On the other hand if we realise its reality it provides a confidence and comfort to our daily living. In this adventure the humdrum is no longer something very ordinary; it becomes part of our great adventure story which begins and ends with God.

17 *Home*

Keep the home-fires burning was the theme of a song whose sentiments are well worth preserving. So many today let them go out. Yet there are few if any institutions which are a greater source of happiness than a good home. There we have our roots. There we learn what love is. And love is the source of the happiness of a home. Without love, life becomes miserable. This love begins with the parents for each other and then goes from them to their children. The children in their turn return the love. Laurence Olivier said: 'I know nothing more beautiful than to set off from home in the morning and to look back and see your young held to a window and waving to you. Its sentimental and its corny, but it's better than poetry, better than genius, better than money.' Love is the most powerful force in the world and it is found at its best in the home.

18 *Disappointments*

We all encounter disappointments in life. There are events we look forward to and which never take place. Rain may spoil a good game of cricket; a friend we were longing to see doesn't turn up. There are plenty of such occasions. Sometimes disappointments arise from more serious reasons. We were perhaps expecting a good rise in salary and it remains where it was. There can be a number of ways in which we react to these situations. We can resent them, grow angry or allow ourselves to become depressed. But the best way surely is to face up to them with courage. A Christian way of regarding disappointments is to see in them an appointment by God. They are part of life and God's providence is not absent from them.

19 *Words of Power*

The Eucharistic words spoken by Christ before His death have created images of beauty in men's minds such as no

R.P.M.—M

other words have ever done. There are no other words in the history of the world which have had a greater impact upon culture and civilisation. Their power has been enormous. Those few simple words spoken over bread and wine have inspired countless artistic creations down the centuries. Music, painting, sculpture, writing, drama would be immensely impoverished without them. Magnificent cathedrals, abbeys, churches, innumerable splendid buildings would never have existed if those words had not been spoken. They have raised men's minds to the wonder, mystery and beauty of the world. They have inspired them to dedicate their lives so that the words would continue to be spoken with power. Those few words of Christ have made the human heart sing and brought home to the mind the lovely things of God's creation and the greater loveliness that lies behind them.

20 *Heaven*

John Donne wrote: 'He that askes me what heaven is, meanes not to heare me but to silence me; he knows I cannot tell him. When I meet him there I shall be able to tell him, and then he will be able to tell me; then we shall be able to tell one another. This, this that we enjoy is heaven, but the tongues of angels, the tongues of glorified saints, shall not be able to express what that heaven is.'

God is perfect truth and love and Heaven consists of possessing this all truth and love; but for us on earth this remains a mystery because we cannot understand what these terms mean as applied to God. We are restless in this life for truth and for love; we know for certain that we will have perfect peace in the next.

21 *Dying*

What is dying? I am standing on the sea shore. A ship sails in the morning breeze and starts for the ocean. She is an object of beauty and I stand watching her till at last she fades on the horizon and someone at my side says 'She is gone'. Gone where? Gone from my sight, that is all; she is just as large in the masts, hull and spars as she was when I saw her, and just as able to bear her load of living freight to its destination. The diminished size and total loss of sight is in me, not in her; and just at the moment when someone at my side says 'She is gone', there are others watching her coming and other voices take up a glad shout: 'There she comes' and that is dying.

BISHOP BRENT 1862–1929

22 *The Conversion of King Edwin*

O King, when we compare the present life of man upon earth with the unknown time before us, it appears to me like the flight of a sparrow passing swiftly through the hall where you recline with your warrior chieftains and your counsellors. A fire is burning brightly in the hall spreading its warmth about it while outside furious storms of snow and rain rage. The sparrow flies swiftly through the hall coming in at one door and going out at the other. For the short time he is inside he is safe from the Wintry tempest but those few moments of calm and comfort are soon over. From the darkness he came and into darkness returned and is lost to human eyes. So too man. Life appears on earth for a short time but we are ignorant of what went before his life, and what comes after. Therefore if this new doctrine brings us more light on the matter it would be right and just that we should follow it.

THE VENERABLE BEDE c. 673–735

23 *Morality*

President Theodore Roosevelt said: 'When you educate a man in mind and not in morals you educate a menace to society. Science is learning to control much, but we have not solved the problems of hate, lust, greed and prejudice which produce social injustice, racial strife and ultimately war. A nation cannot afford to neglect its spiritual and moral life otherwise it will disintegrate.'

Christianity did not set up a complete new code of morality. What it did do was to supply an incentive and a purpose for following the moral law. For morality to be an effective basis for living it must be inspired by faith. Morality for its own sake alone appeals to few people.

24 *The Great Fall*

The nursery rhyme, Humpty-dumpty, is a parable of mankind who had a great fall. Somewhere buried in the history of the human race, evil entered and brought havoc. All the king's horses, all the efforts of men could not restore wholeness to them. Man's fall made him helpless. He lay like the man in the Gospels who was attacked by robbers. He needed the good services of a Samaritan to bring him back to health. Only God could do it. The way He did it was unnecessary, except that His love seemed to make it so. He lifted men up with His Son on a cross to die and then gave them a life with new powers when with Christ they rose to life.

25 *The Death of the Venerable Bede*

Two weeks before Easter in the year 735, the Venerable Bede grew very weak though he still taught his scholars and chanted psalms daily and spent hours in prayer at night. He desired to complete a translation of St John's Gospel into English. His boy secretary, Wilbert, whom he kept by his side said: 'There is only one chapter left in the book you have been dictating.' In the afternoon he sent for the priests of the house and distributed among them his few possessions imploring them to be diligent in saying Masses and prayers for him and as they wept at the thought of his dying he told them that his soul longed to see 'Christ, my king, in his beauty.' Evening came and the boy Wilbert said: 'Dear master, there is only one sentence more not written down.' 'It is well,' he said, 'write it.' In a short while the boy said: 'Now it is finished.' Then, as he lay on the floor of his cell he chanted the Gloria Patri and as he chanted it he died.

26 *Prayer to Christ Crucified*

My tongue shall be my pen, mine eyes shall rain
Tears for my ink, the cross where I was cur'd
Shall be my book, where having all abjured
And calling heavens to record in that plaine
Thus plainely will I write: no sin like mine.
When I have done, do thou Jesu divine
Take up the tart sponge of thy Passion
And blot it forth; then be thy spirit the Quill
Thy blood the Ink, and with compassion
Write thus upon my soul thy Jesu still.

WILLIAM ALABASTER 1567–1640

27 *A Walk in the Country*

I went out one afternoon for a walk alone. I was in the empty unthinking state in which one saunters along country lanes, simply yielding oneself to the casual sights around which give a town-bred lad with country yearnings such intense delight. Suddenly I became conscious of the presence of someone else. I cannot describe it, but I felt that I had as direct perception of the being of God all around about me as I have of you when we are together. It was no longer a matter of influence it was an immediate act of spiritual (or whatever adjective you like to employ) apprehension. It came unsought, absolutely unexpectedly. I remember the wonderful transfiguration of the far-off woods and hills as this seemed to blend in the infinite being with which I was thus brought into relation. This experience did not last long. But it sufficed to change all my feeling. I had not found God because I had not looked for Him. But He had found me.

J. E. CARPENTER 1813–1885

28 *Sunrise*

Morning awakes; glad earth and sky
Smile in the splendour of the day begun.
O'er the broad earth's illumined canopy,
Shade of its Maker's majesty, the sun
Gleams in its living light from cloud to cloud;
Streaks of all colours beautifully run
As if before heaven's gate there hung a shroud
To hide its grand magnificence, O heaven,
Where entrance e'en to thought is disallowed,
To view the glory that this scene is giving
What may blind reason not expect to see,
When in immortal worlds the soul is living
Eternal as its maker, and as free
To taste the unknown of eternity?

JOHN CLARE 1793–1864

29 *St Augustine and Love*

Not with doubting, but with assured consciousness, do I love Thee, Lord. Thou has stricken my heart with Thy word, and I loved Thee. Yea also heaven and earth and all

193

that is therein bid me love Thee … But what do I love when I love Thee? Not beauty of bodies, nor the fair harmony of time, nor the brightness of light, so gladsome to our eyes, nor sweet melodies of varied songs, nor the fragrant smell of flowers and ointment and spices, not manna and honey, not limbs acceptable to embracement of flesh. None of these things do I love when I love my God: and yet I love a kind of light, and melody and fragrance, and meat and embracement, when I love my God, the light, melody, fragrance, meat, embracement of my inner man: where there shines into my soul what space cannot contain, and there sounds what time does not bear away, and there smells what breathing does not disperse, and there tastes what eating does not diminish, and there clings what satiety does not divorce. This it is which I love when I love my God.

30 *The Graveyard*

George Gissing in his book, *Demos*, gives a very beautiful but sad picture of an East End graveyard. Life's struggles and labours are over and here is rest. 'Here lie those who were born for toil; who, when toil has worn them to the uttermost, have but to yield their useless breath and pass into oblivion. For them there is no day, only a brief twilight of a winter sky between the former and the latter night. The wind sails above the narrow tenements; the sandy soil, soaking in the rain as soon as it is fallen, is a symbol of the great world which absorbs their toil and straightway blots their being.'

There is a finality about those words; life is ended. How different is a Christian graveyard 'I am the Resurrection and the Life, he who believes in me will live for ever.'

October

1 *The Door in the Wall*

In the story, *The Door in the Wall*, by H. G. Wells, a small six-year-old boy, wandering through the streets of London, comēs to a green door in a white wall. He opens it and sees a wonderful enchanting garden stretching out to the horizon. An old woman shows him a book in which he sees himself and all that has happened to him since he was born. Then the old woman bends down and kisses him and immediately he finds himself crying in a long street in London. Many times afterwards he tries to find the door in the wall again but could not do so.

That story is a parable of human endeavour. People grow restless in their search for peace and happiness. They are looking for the door in the wall through which they will find fulfilment. They all want the enchanting garden but so many are looking in the wrong places. Christ said: 'I am the door.' It is through that door that perfect peace and happiness will be found.

2 *Faith and Reason*

Pascal wrote: 'If we submit everything to the test of reason, our religion will have nothing of mystery or of the supernatural about it. If our religion violates the rules of reason, it will be absurd and it will be rightly ridiculed.'

Faith is not the same as intellectual conviction; it is not the end result of a logical process, the conclusion to a syllogism. Reason leads up to it but always there is a final leap in the dark, a surrender of the intellect to God and at the same time an acceptance that this is right and reasonable.

'Understanding is the reward of faith,' wrote St Augustine, 'therefore seek not to understand that thou mayest believe but believe that thou mayest understand.'

3 *Progress*

We live in an age in which evolutionary ideas tend to dominate many human minds. There are those who think that we are all the time progressing towards a better world and a more united one because of the advances that science and technology have made. But the shadow of the nuclear bomb, the increase in all kinds of weapons of war, the germs in our national laboratories, make this type of thinking questionable. There can be no real progress or union of mankind if the spiritual life of man is neglected. Carlyle expressed this well when he said: 'The misfortune of man has its source in his greatness; for there is something infinite in him, and he cannot succeed in burying himself completely in the finite.'

4 *The Light of the Spirit*

Ah! From the soul itself must issue forth
A light, a glory, a fair luminous cloud
Enveloping the earth.
And from the soul itself must there be sent
A sweet and potent voice, of its own birth,
Of all sweet sounds the life and element.
O pure of heart! Thou need'st not ask of me

What this strong music in the soul may be.
What, and wherein it doth exist,
This light, this glory, this fair luminous mist
This beautiful and beauty-making power.

The poet Coleridge's words can very aptly be applied to the presence of the Spirit of light in a human soul, a light that does 'issue forth' in goodness of life. The Christian must be 'a beauty-making power' by shedding the light of truth about him; a light which is a reflection of the light of the Spirit within him.

5 *From a Sermon*

No man is an island, entire of itself, every man is a piece of the continent, a part of the main. If a clod be washed away by the sea, Europe is the less, as well as if a promontory were, as well as if a manor of thy friend's or of thine own were; any man's death diminishes me, because I am involved in mankind; and therefore never send to know for whom the bell tolls; it tolls for thee. Neither can we call this a begging of misery, or borrowing of misery, as though we were not miserable enough of ourselves, but must fetch in more from the next house, in taking upon us the misery of our neighbours. Truly it were an excusable covetousness if we did, for affliction is a treasure, and scarce any man has enough of it. No man hath affliction enough that is not matured and ripened by it, and made fit for God by that affliction.

JOHN DONNE 1572–1631

6 *The Thread of Life*

The irresponsive silence of the land,
The irresponsive sounding of the sea,
Speak both one message of one sense to me:–
Aloof, aloof, we stand aloof, so stand
Thou too aloof bound with the flawless band
Of inner solitude; we bind not thee;
But who from thy self-chain shall set thee free?
What heart shall touch thy heart? What hand thy hand?
And I am sometimes proud and sometimes meek,
And sometimes I remember days of old
When fellowship seemed not so far to seek
And all the world and I seemed much less cold,
And at the rainbow's foot lay surely gold,
And hope felt strong and life itself not weak.

CHRISTINA GEORGINA ROSSETTI 1830–1894

7 *The Power of Divinity*

The wonderful thing about the sense of divinity as it appears in Jesus is its naturalness, the absence of surprise or of any feeling of violence. We might have said beforehand, if we had been told that God was coming into a man's life – we might have said, that must be something very terrible and awful. That certainly must rend and tear the life to which God comes. At least it will separate it and make it unnatural and strange. God fills a bush with His glory and it burns. God enters into the great mountain and it rocks with earthquakes. When He comes to occupy a man He must distort the humanity which he occupies into some inhuman shape. Instead of that, this new life into which God comes seems to be the most quietly, naturally human life that was ever seen upon the earth. It glides into its place like sunlight. It seems to make it evident that God and man are essentially so near together that the meeting of their natures in the life of the God-man is not strange.

BISHOP PHILLIPS BROOKS 1835–1893

8 *Love*

Love bade me welcome: yet my soul drew back
Guiltie of dust and sinne.
But quick-ey'd Love, observing me grow slack
From my first entrance in,
Drew nearer to me, sweetly questioning,
If I lack'd any thing.

A guest, I answer'd, worthy to be here:
Love said, You shall be he
I the unkinde, ungratefull? Ah my deare,
I cannot look on thee.
Love took my hand, and smiling did reply
Who made the eyes but I?

Truth, Lord, but I have marr'd them: let my shame
Go where it doth deserve.
And know you not, sayes Love, who bore the blame?
My deare, then I will serve.
You must sit down, sayes Love, and taste my meat:
So I did sit and eat.

GEORGE HERBERT 1593–1633

9 *How to enjoy the World*

You never enjoy the world aright till the sea itself floweth in your veins, till you are clothed with the heavens, and crowned with the stars; and perceive yourself to be the sole heir of the whole world; and more so then, because men are in it who are every one sole heirs, as well as you. Till you can sing and rejoice and delight in God, as misers do in gold, and kings in sceptres, you never enjoy the world.

THOMAS TRAHERNE c. 1637–1674

10 *Happiness in the World*

I feel that a man may be happy in this world and I know that this world is a world of imagination and vision. I see everything I paint in this world but everybody does not see alike. To the eye of a miser a guinea is far more beautiful than the sun and a bag worn with the use of money has more beautiful proportions than a vine filled with grapes. The tree which moves some to tears of joy is in the eyes of others only a green thing which stands in the way. As a man is, so he sees. When the sun rises, do you not see a round disk of fire something like a gold piece? Oh no, no, I see an innumerable company of the heavenly host crying Holy, Holy, Holy is the Lord God almighty. I do not question my bodily eye any more than I would question a window concerning sight. I look through it and not with it.

WILLIAM BLAKE 1757–1827

11 *Advice from a Lawyer*

Max Ehrmann wrote this in 1927: 'Be yourself. Especially do not feign affection. Neither be cynical about love; for in the face of all disenchantment it is perennial as the grass. Take kindly the counsel of the years, gracefully surrendering the things of youth. Nurture strength of spirit to shield you in misfortune. But do not distress yourself with imaginings. Many fears are born of fatigue and loneliness. Beyond a wholesome discipline, be gentle with yourself.

'You are a child of the universe, no less than the trees and the stars; you have a right to be here. And whether or not it is clear to you, no doubt the universe is unfolding as it should. Therefore be at peace with God, whatever you conceive Him to be, and whatever your labours and aspirations, in the noisy confusion of life, keep peace with your soul. With all its sham, drudgery and broken dreams, it is still a beautiful world. Be careful. Strive to be happy.'

12 *St Augustine talks with his Mother*

Sweet was the converse we held together, as forgetting those things which were behind, and reaching forth unto those things which were before, we asked ourselves in the presence of Thee, the Truth, what will be the manner of the eternal life of the saints, which eye has not seen, nor ear heard, neither has it entered into the heart of man? And as our converse drew to this conclusion, that the sweetest conceivable delight of sense in the brightest conceivable earthly sunshine was not to be compared with the happiness of that life, we soared with glowing hearts towards the same, mounting step-by-step the ladder of the material order through heaven itself, whence sun and moon and stars shed their radiance upon earth. And still higher did we climb by the staircase of the spirit, thinking and speaking of Thee, and marvelling at Thy works ... Suppose we heard Him without any intermediary at all. Just now we reached out, and with one flash of thought, touched the Eternal Wisdom that abides above all – is not this the meaning of 'Enter into the joy of thy Lord'?

13 *The Advertisement of Love*

The cross is the advertisement of God's love. It is dug into the earth so that its mysterious power can penetrate and pervade it and thus give reality to all that happens on its surface. So love and suffering and joy and all the pageant of human activities are given substance and significance through it and all the peoples of the world can find in it reconciliation and peace. But why must love advertise itself through suffering? Why a cross rather than a throne? Why thorns and not a crown? Must God be mocked and spat upon for men to respond with love? Must he be put on trial and have sentence passed on him in order that love may give evidence of its presence? All this is high mystery. And yet can one think of a better way of advertising love? After all He said Himself: 'If I be lifted up from the earth I will draw all men to myself.' Suffering has a drawing power and when the suffering is divine its force is all powerful.

14 *The Conquest of the Cross*

Christ intimated that it would be through the cross that He would conquer and win the world over to Himself. We have only to look back and see the magnetic force of that sign dug in the earth, how it has penetrated the world and drawn millions of men and women to itself, to see how true Christ's words have been. Love demands love. And countless men and women have brought their sufferings and trials and united them to His in great acts of love. They have come with the knowledge that behind the crucifixion is the glory and light of a splendid resurrection.

For the death of the Son of God on a cross waas the resurrection of men's hopes and a realisation that in Him and through Him they would have eternal love. For the cross would not always be plunged in the darkness of Golgotha – after the night would come the bright dawn – through the agony would come the joy – through the desolation and the pain would arise the splendour of an awakening to glory which would never depart.

15 *The Pulley*

> When God at first made man,
> Having a glass of blessings standing by,
> 'Let us', said He, 'pour on him all we can;
> Let the world's riches, which dispersèd lie,
> Contract into a span.'
>
> So strength first made a way,
> Then beauty flowed, then wisdom, honour pleasure;

When almost all was out, God made a stay,
Perceiving that, alone of all His treasure,
Rest in the bottom lay.

'For if I should,' said He,
'Bestow this jewel also on my creatures,
He would adore my gifts instead of me,
And rest in Nature, not the God of Nature;
So both should losers be.

Yet let him keep the rest,
But keep them with repining restlessness;
Let him be rich and weary, that at least,
If goodness lead him not, yet weariness
May toss him to my breast.

GEORGE HERBERT 1593–1633

16 *Patriotism*

In the summer of 1936 during the Spanish Civil War, the Alcazar at Toledo was beleaguered by the 'Reds'. In the Alcazar the cadets, under the leadership of General Moscardo, remained loyal to Spain. They defended the Alcazar, under machine-gun fire and exploding mines and bombs, for ten long weeks till they were relieved by the National troops. Moscardo spoke to the 'Reds', who held his son prisoner, by field telephone. They said they would shoot his son if he did not surrender. The general replied that he would not yield and his son was shot.

On the wall of the Alcazar today there is a tablet bearing the words of father to son in their last conversation: 'My son, God receive your soul, cry "Long live Spain" and die like a patriot.'

17 *Resolution*

But what if I fail of my purpose here? –
It is but to keep the nerves at strain,
To dry one's eyes and laugh at a fall,
And baffled, get up to begin again, –
So the chance takes up one's life, that's all.
While, look but once from your farthest bound,
at me so deep in the dust and dark,
No sooner the old hope drops to ground
Than a new one, straight to the selfsame mark,
   I shape me –
   Ever
      Removed!

ROBERT BROWNING 1812–1889

18 *The Rainbow*

Ishmael in Herman Melville's *Moby Dick* watches the rainbow formed amid the spray sprouting from the hunted whale and sees in it a mystical quality. 'For d'ye see rainbows do not visit the clear air; they only irradiate vapour. And so, through all the thick mists of the dim doubts in my mind, divine intuitions now and then shoot, enkindling my fog with heavenly ray. And for this I thank God; for all have doubts; many deny; but doubts or denial, few along with them, have intuitions. Doubts of all things earthly, and intuitions of some things heavenly; this combination makes neither believer or infidel, but makes a man who regards them both with equal eye.'

19 *Christ's Little Ones*

This is what it is to be one of Christ's little ones ... to be possessed by His presence as our life, our strength, our merit, our hope, our crown; to become in a wonderful way His members, the instruments or visible form or sacramental sign of the one invisible ever-present Son of God, mystically reiterating in each of us all the acts of His earthly life, His birth, consecration, fasting, temptation, conflicts, victories, sufferings, agony, passion, death, resurrection and ascension:– He being all in all – we, with as little power in ourselves, as little excellence or merit, as the water in Baptism, or the bread and wine in holy Communion; yet strong in the Lord and in the power of His might.

CARDINAL NEWMAN 1801–1890

20 *God's Purpose with Men*

St Paul is never tired of contemplating the mystery of God's purposes with men 'in the dispensation of the fulness of time to re-establish all things in Christ that are in heaven and on earth.' This is a magnificent vision of the role of Christ.

It captivated the mind and imagination of Teilhard de Chardin who wrote: 'Like lightning, like a conflagration, like a flood, the attraction exerted by the Son of Man will lay hold of the whirling elements in the universe so as to reunite them or subject them to His body.'

We must never forget that Christ came not only to save the world but also to fulfil it. He came to give it significance and also to bring it under His influence so that He would 'subject all things under his feet'. We should see the first coming of Christ into our world in terms of a second when His work of Saviour will have been completed. This second coming will make clear the significance of the first. It will reveal Christ's impact upon history and on the personal lives of men.

21 *The Legend*

There is a beautiful legend which relates that the god Apollo laid down his lyre upon a stone and the dumb rock absorbed the dying strains of the melody. Whoever would find this stone, could, if he placed it to his ear, hear the slumbering song of the Olympic god. Just as in the strings of a violin or in the bronze of a bell, the melodies sleep until they are awakened, so in every human soul there lies dormant a note of divinity. There is God within us all but He must be awakened for us by our faith and devotion. His presence must become real for us by prayer.

22 *The Daisy*

Slight as thou art, thou art enough to hide,
Like all created things, secrets from me,
And stand a barrier to eternity.
And I, how can I praise thee well and wide
From whence I dwell upon the other side?
Thou little veil of so great mystery,
When shall I penetrate all things and thee
And then look back?   ALICE MEYNELL 1847–1922

23 *The Joy of Work*

Give us, oh, give us, the man who sings at his work. He will do more in the same time – he will do it better – he will persevere longer. One is scarcely sensible of fatigue whilst he marches to music. The very stars are said to make harmony as they revolve in their spheres. Wondrous is the strength of cheerfulness, altogether past calculation in its power of endurance. Efforts, to be permanently useful, must be uniformly joyous, a spirit all sunshine and graceful from very gladness, beautiful because bright.

THOMAS CARLYLE 1795–1881

24 *Peace*

I seek for peace – I care not where 'tis found
On this rude scene in briars and brambles drest,
If peace dwells here, 'tis consecrated ground,
And owns the power to give my bosom rest;
To soothe the rankling of each bitter wound.
Gall'd by rude envy's adder-biting jest,
And worldly strife – ah, I am looking round
For peace's hermitage, can it be found?
Surely that breeze that o'er the blue wave curl'd
Did whisper soft, 'Thy wanderings here are blest.'
How different from the language of the world!
Nor jeers nor taunts in this still spot are given;
Its calm's a balsam to a soul distrest;
And, where peace smiles, a wilderness is heaven.

JOHN CLARE 1793–1864

25 *The Cloud of Unknowing*

All rational beings, angels and men, possess two faculties, the power of knowing and the power of loving. To the first, to the intellect, God who made them is forever unknowable, but to the second, to love, He is completely knowable, and that by every separate individual. So much so that one loving soul by itself, through His love, may know for itself Him who is incomparably more than sufficient to fill all souls that exist. This is the everlasting miracle of love, for God works in this fashion and always will. Consider this, if by God's grace you are able to, to know it for oneself is endless bliss; its contrary to endless pain.

26 *A Wish to God*

I would to God that mine old age might have
Before my last, but here a living grave,
Some one poor alms-house, there to lie, or stir
Ghost-like, as in my meaner sepulchre;
A little piggin, and a pipklin by,
To hold things fitting my necessity;
Which, rightly used, both in their time and place,
Might me excite to fore, and after – grace;
Thy cross, my Christ, fixed 'fore mine eyes should be,
Not to adore that, but to worship Thee.
So here the remnant of my days I'd spend
Reading Thy bible, and my book; so end.

ROBERT HERRICK 1591–1674

27 *The Emerald*

In St Ninian's cathedral, Perth, one of the chalices has at its base a magnificent emerald. Close to it is a note which identifies the stone as 'formerly the eye of an Indian god'. The purpose of the gem has been transformed so that now it is consecrated to the service of the true God. It now forms part of a chalice which will hold wine to be consecrated and become the blood of Christ. At Cana water became wine at the word of Christ. What was a very ordinary substance took on a precious form. This happens continually in our world because of Christ. Ordinary everyday activities, simple and commonplace in themselves become precious in the eyes of God when done for Him with love. The smallest things we do become enriched when we make of them an offering to God.

28 *I will Arise*

When Christopher Wren stood amid the ruins of the old St Paul's cathedral which had been burnt down, he asked a workman to fetch him a stone to mark the centre of the new cathedral. The man brought him a fragment of a gravestone on which was engraved one word 'Resurgam', I will arise.

The present St Paul's is that resurrection – a new building on the ruins of the old – life after death. Resurrection means hope. A future coming out of a dead past. Resurrection is at the heart of Christianity. What may seem dead in our lives because of sorrow or pain will make way for a resurrection of joy. Just as the daylight comes after a dark night so will it be with us. United with Christ the Winter of our troubled life will make way for an eternal Spring; the darkness will be followed by the brightness of everlasting light.

29 *The Kindness of the Spirit*

There are those who get a morbid thrill from watching the agony of others. They are like those who used to flock to public executions or those described in John Masefield's poem:

> There was a group outside the prison gate
> Waiting to hear them ring the passing bell,
> Waiting as empty people always wait
> For the strong toxin of another's hell.

Human nature left to itself can be very cruel. Oscar Wilde experienced this as he waited on the station platform in convict dress. People jeered and laughed at him: 'For half an hour I stood there in the grey November rain surrounded by a jeering mob.' If those who jeered had been filled with the Spirit how different their reaction would have been. There is a warmth and glow in life when the Spirit is present, a warmth which radiates outward to others.

30 *Kindness to Others*

Everyone has something to contribute to the happiness of the world and no matter how small and insignificant it may seem, it can be of value in furthering that end. Kindness to others is kindness to self because it makes the heart expand and brings a sense of achievement and self-realisation. Wordsworth wrote of 'that best portion of a good man's life; his little nameless, unremembered acts of kindness and love.' St Paul tells us the origin of these kindly acts of love: 'God's love has been poured into our hearts through the Holy Spirit that has been given to us.'

All kindness is a reflection of the kindness of God. There is nothing good in the human heart which does not come from God through His Spirit. This is true even of those who do not recognise or acknowledge it.

31 *Delight in Nature*

First saw the Northern Lights. My eye was caught by beams of light and dark very like the crown of horny rays the sun makes behind a cloud. At first I thought of silvery cloud until I saw that these were more luminous and did not dim the clearness of the stars in the Bear. They rose slightly radiating thrown out from the earthline. Then I saw soft pulses of light one after another rise and pass upwards arched in shape but waveringly and with the arch broken. They seemed to float, not following the warp of the sphere as falling stars look to do but free though concentrical with it. This busy working of Nature wholly independent of the earth and seeming to go on in a strain of time not reckoned by our reckoning of days and years but simpler and as if correcting the preoccupation of the world by being preoccupied with and appealing to and dated to the day of judgement was like a new witness to God and filled me with delightful fear.

GERARD MANLEY HOPKINS 1844–1889

November

1 *Feast of All Saints*

Those who have visited Rome will not have failed to see the Pantheon. This great circular building with its huge dome was built in the reign of the Emperor Augustus, the emperor who reigned when Christ was born, and dedicated as a temple to all the gods. Later it became a Christian church and Pope Boniface IV dedicated it to the blessed Virgin and all the martyrs, inspired, no doubt, by the desire that instead of the idolatrous worship of false gods, there would be the veneration of the mother of the true God and all his saints. In this way the festival of All Saints had its origin in the Western church in Rome. In the middle of the ninth century the feast spread to the universal church.

2 *A Prayer*

An unknown soldier in the American Civil War wrote the following prayer:

> I asked God for strength, that I might achieve,
> I was made weak, that I might learn humbly to obey . . .
> I asked for health, that I might do greater things,
> I was given infirmity, that I might do better things . . .
> I asked for riches, that I might be happy,
> I was given poverty, that I might be wise . . .
> I asked for power, that I might have the praise of men,
> I was given weakness, that I might feel the need of
>   God . . .
> I asked for all things, that I might enjoy life,
> I was given life, that I might enjoy all things . . .

I got nothing that I asked for, but everything I had
    hoped for
Almost despite myself, my unspoken prayers were
    answered.
I am among all men, most richly blessed.

3 *The Scales of Justice*

Sometimes carved on some mediaeval cathedral or illustrated in some ancient prayer book are pictures of the
scales of justice. In front of some trembling sinner a grin-
ning devil is loading one side of the scales with the sins of a
lifetime while on the other, an angel is placing the virtuous
actions. What an awful moment in our existence it would
be if this kind of thing actually happened. What a shiver
would penetrate our being as we watched all the lies, the
uncharitable thoughts and actions, the jealousies and
hatreds, the daily *clapper-clawing* go on the scales to be
weighed against our poor virtues. Fortunately our fate does
not depend upon what we did twenty or thirty years ago or
even five minutes ago. It depends solely upon what we are
like at the last moment of our existence. Like the thief on
the cross we can wipe away all our past iniquity by a sincere act of repentance.

4 *The Procession of Palms*

The triumphant ride that Christ made to the temple at Jerusalem was one of great glory. The cries of Hosanna and the

waving of palms exemplified this. But this glory was only a faint glimmer of the true glory which was to be revealed by His coming death. The shouts of applause would soon become cries of scorn and mockery. The poet wrote:

> Not in the clamour of the crowded street,
> Not in the shouts of plaudits of the throng,
> But in ourselves are triumph and defeat.

The triumph of Christ was not in those few waving palms and shouts. He knew that 'the head which today grows giddy with the roar of the million, may tomorrow be fixed upon a pole.' Christ was not carried away by the adulation of the people. It pleased Him but He knew that the real triumph lay in Himself in His 'face set towards Jerusalem' where He would die for His people.

5 *Darkness and Light*

For many a Christian the darkest hour of his life has been one of his greatest hope and joy. How many of those who lived amid the horrors of Belsen, Dachau or some other Nazi concentration camp were able to face death with peace and even joy because of their faith. To take but one example: Father Joseph Muller was arrested on 11 May 1944 and executed on 11 September 1944. On the day of his death he wrote: 'Now my last earthly greeting comes to you from my cell. What shall I say in the circumstances? Oh my heart is so full of joy now that I am on my way home to the Father. I have known all these days that my sacrifice would be accepted. It is now eleven-thirty. In one hour I shall be at home; I shall have left you so far as this earth goes, but nothing can separate us from the love of Christ.' Muller's last prayer, said in Latin, was: 'Know that today the Lord comes and that today you shall see His glory and there shall be a great light on this day I trust in Thee, O Lord, in eternity I shall not be confounded. I believe in the life eternal.'

6 *I Am*

I am! yet what I am who cares, or knows?
My friends forsake me like a memory lost.
I am the self-consumer of my woes;
They rise and vanish, an oblivious host,
Shadows of life, whose very soul is lost.
And yet I am – I live – though I am tossed
Into the nothingness of scorn and noise,
Into the living sea of waking dream,
Where there is neither sense of life, nor joys,
But the huge shipwreck of my own esteem
And all that's dear. Even those I loved the best
Are strange – nay, they are stranger than the rest.

I long for scenes where man has never trod –
For scenes where woman never smiled or wept –
There to abide with my Creator, God,
And sleep as I in childhood sweetly slept,
Full of high thoughts, unborn. So let me lie, –
the grass below; above, the vaulted sky.

JOHN CLARE 1793–1864

7 *Stillness*

Let your mind be quiet, realising the beauty of the world, and the immense the boundless treasures that it holds in store. All that you have within you, all that your heart desires, all that your Nature so especially fits you for – that or the counterpart of it waits embedded in the great Whole for you. It will surely come to you. Yet equally surely not one moment before its appointed time will it come. All your crying and fever and reaching out of hands will make no difference. Therefore do not begin that game at all. Do not recklessly spill the waters of your mind in this direction and in that, lest you become like a spring lost and dissipated in the desert. But draw them together into a little compass, and hold them still, so still; And let them become clear, so clear – so limpid, so mirror-like.

EDWARD CARPENTER 1844–1929

8 *The Shekinah*

Christ is the Shekinah of the New Law. The Shekinah was the manifestation of God's presence and glory. When Solomon dedicated the temple we are told that: 'The whole of the Lord's house was wreathed in cloud: ... His own glory was there, filling His own house. Where the cloud is, cried Solomon, the Lord has promised to be.'

Christ is the glory of God, the brightness of His substance. Like the cloud He hides the full brightness of God's majesty while at the same time He indicates the presence of God within Himself, the temple not made with hands. The beauty and strength of His character were obvious for all to see; there was nothing mysterious about it; yet it was an intimation of a beauty and a power that no sight or imagination could conceive.

9 *Change of Heart*

The Russian writer Tolstoy tells of a time in his life when it seemed to him that his existence had no meaning. 'My life had come to a stop ... there was no real life in me because I had not a single desire, the fulfilment of which I could find to be reasonable ... the idea of suicide came as naturally to me as formerly that of bettering my life.'

Yet later he could write: 'Five years ago I came to believe in Christ's teaching and my life suddenly changed; I ceased to desire what I had previously desired, and began to desire what I formerly did not want. What had previously seemed to me good seemed evil, and what had seemed evil seemed good. It happened to me as it happens to a man who goes out on some business and on the way suddenly decides that the business is unnecessary and returns home. All that was on his right hand is now on his left, and all that was on his left hand is now on his right.'

10 *The Unknown God*

A Hindu writer, Dadu, wrote: 'God cannot be known by mere exercise of intellect. The only way to know God is to cherish an intense desire to realise his true nature, and constantly to be mindful of him. The most indispensable requisite is to purify the mind by keeping it fixed on him and by doing good to others. So long as the mirror is unclean the image cannot be reflected in it.'

Richard Rolle wrote in *The Fire of Love:* 'Thou askest what God is? I answer shortly to thee He is so great that none other is or ever may be of like kind … If thou wilt know properly to speak what God is. I say thou shall never find an answer to this question … How wouldest thou know what is unknown? If thou knew that God is thou shouldest be as wise as God … If thou desirest to know what God is, thou desirest to be God … It is enough for thee to know that God is.'

11 *We Wear the Mask*

We wear the mask that grins and lies
It hides our cheeks and shades our eyes –
This debt we pay to human guile;
With torn and bleeding hearts we smile
And mouth with myriad subtleties.

Why should the world be over-wise
In counting all our tears and sighs?
Nay, let them only see us, while
We wear the mask.

We smile, but, O great Christ, our cries
To thee from tortured souls arise,
We sing, but oh the clay is vile
Beneath our feet, and long the mile;
But let the world dream otherwise,
We wear the mask

PAUL LAURENCE DUNBAR 1877–1906

12 *Man of Peace*

Gandhi wrote: I am a man of peace. I believe in peace. But I do not want peace at any price. I do not want peace that you find in stone; I do not want the peace you find in the grave, but I do want the peace which you find embedded in the human breast, which is exposed to the arrows of the whole world, but which is protected from all harm by the power of Almighty God. My religion is based on truth and non-violence. Truth is my God and non-violence is the means to reach him.

13 *West London*

Crouched on the pavement close by Belgrave Square
A tramp I saw, ill, moody, and tongue-tied
A babe was in her arms, and at her side
A girl, their clothes were rags, their feet were bare.
Some labouring men whose work lay somewhere there,
Passed oppposite; she touched her girl, who hied
Across and begged, and came back satisfied.
The rich she had let pass with frozen stare,
Thought I: Above her state this spirit towers;
She will not ask of aliens, but of friends,
Of sharers in a common human fate.
She turns from that cold succour, which attends
The unknown little from the unknown great,
And points us to a better time than ours.

MATTHEW ARNOLD 1822–1888

14 *Kindness*

The poet Wordsworth spoke of:

That best portion of a good man's life.
His little, nameless, unremembered acts
Of kindness and love.

A former mayor of New York, La Guardia, sometimes presided at court. One very cold day a trembling old man was brought in accused of stealing a loaf of bread; his family was starving he said. 'I've got to punish you', said the mayor. 'The law makes no exceptions. I can do nothing but sentence you to a fine of 10 dollars.' As he said that he put his hands into his pocket: 'Well, here's the 10 dollars and now I remit the fine. Moreover I'm going to fine everybody in this courtroom 50 cents for living in a town where a man has to steal in order to eat. Collect the fines, Mr Bailiff, and give them to the defendant.' The hat was passed round and an incredulous old man with eyes like stars left the court with 47 dollars and 50 cents.

15 *Repentance*

God is ever ready to forgive wrong-doing. Even the most heinous sins are forgiven if followed by true contrition. There is joy before the angels in Heaven upon one sinner being repentant. Even if a person lives a life for years pursuing his own selfish interests to the exclusion of others and of God, all will be pardoned where there is sincere repentance. The rake's progress may go on. He may misuse all the gifts he has received from his Father, God, abuse his faculties of mind and body, yet if his progress ends with sorrow all will be forgiven. Real sorrow is a wonderful medicine. It is a cure for all evil ills.

> I walked a mile with Pleasure
> She chatted all the way
> But left me none the wiser
> For all she had to say.
>
> I walked a mile with Sorrow
> And ne'er a word said she
> But, Oh the things I learned from her
> When Sorrow walked with me.

16 *The Mystery of the Kingdom*

The kingdom that Christ came to found is a great mystery. It is man's response to Him in the depth of his being, where the power of God operates. It is true that the kingdom may be seen in the outward works of Christian men, in their worship and their charity towards their fellow men. One can see the branches of the vine, the flower and the fruit but one cannot see the hidden forces which makes them possible. One can see people who follow Christ and who are united with Him in action but one cannot see the hidden life which gives the power and the union. The life of Christ like the sap in the branches is ever reaching out into the world attracting men to itself. Its boundaries no man knows since no one can penetrate into the depth of a man's soul. For where grace is there is the power of the kingdom. Its light and strength and beauty radiates through men's actions so that they manifest the glory of God.

17 *The Drama of the Incarnation*

The history of Christ's advent on earth consists of a great drama in which the final act was His glorification but every part in that drama was integral to His saving work. Every moment of His life was redemptive. It was not as though He was continually looking forward to His work of salvation. 'The Kingdom of God is among you', He said.

Certainly Christ's death and resurrection were the climax to the drama. The latter was the happy and glorious ending, the finalisation of the work, the purpose for which it was inaugurated. Yet all that led up to it was part of the sacrament of divine love which released the saving grace to the world. The whole of Christ's life was an act of self-surrender, an offering of Himself to the Father so that men might be glorified in Him.

18 *The Seeking the Divine in Things*

This seeing the divine in things intrigued Mother Juliana of Norwich. She said: 'One day he showed me a little thing the quantitie of a hasel-nutt in the palm of my hand, as me seemed; and it was round as a ball. I looked with the eye of the understanding and thought what may this be? And it was answered "It is all that is made." I marvelled how it might last; for me thought it might sodelie have fallen to naught for littleness. And I was answered in my understanding "It lasteth and ever shall for God loveth it." In this little thing I saw three properties:

> the first that God made it
> the second is that God loveth it
> the third that God keepeth it.'

There is so much in so little because the immensity of God is present in every tiny atom of existence and His presence gives it both significance and worth apart from its natural value.

19 *The Meaning of Suffering*

There are those who say that the world moves forward under its own momentum, that it has no need of God to explain its existence. Some say that suffering is a proof of His non-existence. Neither His omnipotence or His goodness would permit it. But surely the very opposite is true. The fact of suffering is an indication of God's existence. He alone can give meaning to it. Do away with Him and what is one to say to the incurably sick, to the old and the lonely, to those in sorrow for the death of a loved one? What can one say except: 'You've had it. You are unfortunate units in a blind evolutionary movement.'

In other words there is no purpose in suffering without God. The sufferer who accepts God may not be able to see the reason for his particular suffering but he knows there is a good one and he also knows that he can make use of his pain and by prayer transform it.

20 *The Inner Conflict*

'Life is a warfare.' All men are involved in conflict in some form. It may be between their desire and their principles, between their individuality and the society about them, between nature and grace, emotions and reason. Whatever form the conflict takes it can only be resolved through personal hurt and asceticism. Only in this way can human nature be perfected and true greatness attained. Conflict is necessary for man's development. The hedonist would deny this but he himself is the proof of it since the more he clutches at pleasures the more they fade like Autumn flowers leaving only disillusionment. The hedonist knows nothing of the peace formula of love, of the harmony and serenity that real, not spurious love, imparts. Love does not guarantee cessation from pain but it does provide the antidote of courage and comfort. For the Christian the answer then to suffering is love and love in it highest form, the love of God.

21 *Matter and Spirit*

Soul and body – how mysterious their union is. The one can be weighed, chemically analysed, can be seen and felt. The other cannot be demonstrated on any physical or visible basis. The composite of spirit and matter which makes up human personality is among the great mysteries of the world. In the crucible of self are distilled thoughts and emotions that either poison or refine it. The body may be healthy, elegant, perfect in proportions and yet be the receptacle of ugliness and curruption. Such was Dorian Gray in Oscar Wilde's parable; his was an extraordinary personal beauty which was the very antithesis of his vileness of character. This very beauty which he retained all his life in its youthful bloom was the cause of his moral downfall and eventually of his dreadful suicidal death. Outward beauty is of no account unless it is matched by beauty of soul. The body should be like a violin on which the spirit plays so that together they produce a perfect harmony.

22 *The Holy Spirit and Providence*

The activity of the Holy Spirit in human affairs is completely hidden; one's faith can recognise that He is at work. It alone can accept the mystery of the relationship of the Spirit with the human will. It may well be said that civilisation and culture are the results of human endeavour and not of some unseen power. Yet the Holy Spirit is involved. I think that most of us who believe in the power of God over human lives can look back at our own and see the providence of God at work in it. It may be something said, some small incident, some sudden desire, which has had a profound influence on the direction our lives have taken. We have been 'inspired' by them for our good. If we can see this happening in our personal lives why should it not happen in the wider field of human activities? After all, what is it in the end that shapes the world and decides its direction? Surely it is the brain of man and the emotions of his heart, thrusting out into action. Are we to say that the Holy Spirit has played no part in this? Have world religions, for example, not had their impact upon society? To take the supreme example of Christianity; it has diverted the world into completely new channels by creating a culture and civilisation which has affected every nation in it. And we know that the Spirit of God resides in the very heart of Christianity.

23 *The Truth about Suffering*

It was a scene of dramatic irony when Pilate, in sceptical mood, asked: 'What is truth?' of the man standing before him, who was Truth itself.

No-one can blame Pilate for his lack of recognition, only for his scepticism. The 'Truth' was a broken image; blood and sweat and blows had disfigured it, clothing it with a mask of pain. Yet in reality disfigurement and suffering were signatures of the Truth; for it was only through them that the truth about the Truth became fully known. The seed must go into darkness and be broken and shattered if it is to be seen in its full splendour of growth of fruit. There are Pilates of every age who ask the question that he asked and, like him, are sceptical about an answer. Pilate failed to see the truth hidden in suffering; so do the Pilates today. They cannot gasp the truth that it can be written in blood; that it was the blood of Christ that revealed the truth about the world and the lives of those who live in it, that Truth was crucified and through crucifixion gave a meaning to suffering.

24 *Suffering and Hope*

Christ planted in suffering the germ of hope, providing a liberating power so that it would burst the bars of self-imprisonment and make clear that only through suffering in some form can men attain their full perfection. For Christ must be crucified in men if they are to rise again with Him. The thief in his agony recognised the dying Truth and obtained salvation. The misery of the beggar Lazarus rather than the prosperity of the rich man Dives, gained eternal happiness. Ann Frank amid her claustrophobic suffering saw the truth written in the sky from her attic window and thus gained peace of soul. Oscar Wilde in his degradation could write in *E Tenebris*:

> Come down, O Christ, and help me! Reach they hand
> For I am drowning in a stormier sea
> Than Simon on thy lake of Galilee:
> The wine of life is spilt upon the sand
> My heart is as some famine-murdered land,
> Whence all good things have perished utterly
> And well I know my soul in Hell must lie
> If I this night before God's throne should stand.

25 *The Pure of Heart*

There is much talk today of the pollution of our towns and countryside. The atmosphere has become full of pernicious gases, rivers and streams are defiled by industry, streets and roads fouled by rubbish. There is a corresponding danger of pollution of the inner spirit of man. He is surrounded by all kinds of noxious ideas and he lives and moves in an atmosphere injurious to his spiritual health. Christ told the people on the mountainside that those were blessed who were pure of heart, for they would have the vision of God. The pure of heart are those who receive the living water of the Spirit. Such was the woman of Samaria whose heart was cleansed of evil by it so that she saw God in Christ. There can be no true vision without the Spirit. Without Him men are like the blind leading the blind. His presence makes the way ahead clear by dispelling all obstacles to progress.

26 *Words about the Spirit*

Gerard Manley Hopkins wrote: 'A Paraclete is something that cheers the spirit of man with signals and with cries, all zealous that he should do something, full of assurance that if he will he can, calling on him, springing to meet him half-way, crying to his ears or to his heart; this way to do God's will, the way to save your soul, come on, come on.'

Hopkins went on to say how the Spirit played the Paraclete among the apostles: 'First He cheered them on, but He cheered them on not like Christ by His example from without but by His presence, His power, His breath and fire and inspiration from within; not by drawing but by driving; not by shewing them what to do but by Himself within them doing it. His mighty breath ran with roaring in their ears, His fire flamed in tongues upon their foreheads, and their hearts and lips were filled with Himself, with the Holy Ghost.'

27 *Providence*

O sacred Providence who from end to end
Strongly and sweetly movest! Shall I write
And not of Thee, through whom my fingers bend
To hold my quill? shall they not do Thee right?

Of all Thy creatures both in sea and land
Only to man thou hast made known Thy wayes
And put the penne alone into his hand
And made him Secretarie of Thy praise.

All things that are, though they have sev'ral wayes
Yet in their being joyn with one advise
To honour Thee; and so I give Thee praise
In all my other hymnes, but in this twice.

GEORGE HERBERT 1593–1633

28 *War and Peace*

At the inauguration of the Institute Pasteur in 1888, the famous French scientist, Pasteur, closed his address with these words: 'Two opposing laws seem to me now in contest. The one, a law of blood and death, opening out each day new modes of destruction, forces nations to be always ready for the battle. The other, the law of peace, work and health, whose only aim is to deliver man from the calamities that beset him. The one seeks violent conquests, the other the relief of mankind. The one places a single life above all victories, the other sacrifices hundreds of thousands of lives to the ambition of a single individual. The law of which we are the instruments strives even through the carnage to cure the wounds due to the law of war. Treatment by our antiseptic methods may preserve the lives of thousands of soldiers. Which of these two laws will prevail God only knows. But of this we may be sure, that science, in obeying the law of humanity, will always labour to enlarge the frontiers of life.'

29 *Prayer*

Oft have I seen at some cathedral door
A labourer, pausing in the dust and heat,
Lay down his burden, and with reverent feet
Enter, and cross himself, and on the floor
Kneel to repeat his paternoster O'er;
Far off the noises of the world retreat;
The loud vociferations of the street
Become an undistinguishable roar.
So, as I enter here from day to day,
And leave my burden at this minster gate,
Kneeling in prayer, and not ashamed to pray,
The tumult of the time disconsolate
To inarticulate murmurs die away,
While the eternal ages watch and wait.

HENRY WADSWORTH LONGFELLOW 1807–1882

30 *All Embracing Love*

Dostoevsky wrote: 'Love all God's creation, both the whole and every grain of sand. Love every leaf, every ray of light. Love the animals, love the plants, love each separate thing. If you love each thing you will perceive the mystery of God in all; and when once you perceive this, you will henceforward grow every day to a fuller understanding of it: until you come at last to love the whole world with a love that will then be all-embracing and universal.'

December

1 *The Celestial Surgeon*

If I have faltered more or less
In my great task of happiness,
If I have moved among my race
And shown no glorious morning face;
If beams from happy human eyes
Have moved me not; if morning skies
Books, and my food, and summer rain
Knocked on my sullen heart in vain –
Lord, Thy most pointed pleasure take
And stab my spirit broad awake;
Or, Lord, if too obdurate I
choose Thou, before that spirit die,
A piercing pain, a killing sin.
And to my dead heart run them in.

ROBERT LOUIS STEVENSON 1850–1894

2 *Pauses*

In our whole life melody the music is broken off here and there by rests, and we foolishly think we have come to the end of time. God sends a time of forced leisure, a time of sickness and disappointed plans, and makes a sudden pause in the hymns of our lives, and we lament that our voice must be silent and our part missing in the music which ever goes up to the ear of our creator. Not without design does God write the music of our lives. Be it ours to learn the time and not be dismayed at the rests. If we look up, God will beat the time for us.

JOHN RUSKIN 1819–1900

3 Testimony

The third-century martyr, St Cyprian, said: 'This is a cheerful world as I see it from my garden under the shadows of my vines. But if I were to ascend some high mountain and look out over the wide lands, you know very well what I should see: brigands on the highways, pirates on the seas, armies fighting, cities burning; in the amphitheatres men murdered to please applauding mobs; selfishness and cruelty and misery and despair under all roofs. It is a bad world, Donatus, an incredibly bad world. But I have discovered in the midst of it a quiet and holy people who have learned a great secret. They have found a joy which is a thousand times better than any pleasure of our sinful life. They are despised and persecuted but they care not. They are masters of their souls. They have overcome the world. These people, Donatus, are the Christians and I am one of them.'

4 Repentance

In *The Brothers Karamazov* Dostoevsky wrote that before he became a Christian he had no idea what Christian charity demanded. When he was an officer in the army he once struck his orderly. He describes what happened: 'I saw the scene as if it were happening all over again; the poor lad standing in front of me while I struck his face with all my might, his hands on his trouser seams, his head erect, his eyes wide open and trembling at every blow but not daring so much as to raise his arms to shield himself. How can a man be reduced to such a state? To be beaten by another man – what a crime! It was like a needle piercing my soul. I felt as if I had lost my wits and the sun was shining and leaves gave cheer to one's sight and birds were praising the Lord. Lord, can it be true, I thought as I wept, perhaps I am the most wicked of men, the worst there is.'

5 *Unexpected Surprises*

Into all our lives, in many simple, familiar homely ways, God infuses this element of joy from the surprises of life, which unexpectedly brighten our days and fill our eyes with light. He drops the added sweetness into His childrens' cup, and makes it to run over. The success we are not counting on, the blessing we were not trying after, the strain of music in the midst of drudgery, the beautiful morning picture of sunset glory thrown in as we pass to or from our daily business, the unsought word of encouragement of expression of sympathy, the sentence that meant for us more than a writer or speaker thought – these and a hundred others that everyone's experience can supply are instances of what I mean.

SAMUEL LONGFELLOW 1819–1892

6 *True Joy*

Would one think it possible for a man to delight in gauderies like a butterfly and neglect the Heavens? Did we not see it daily, it would be incredible. They rejoice in a piece of gold more than in the sun; and get a few little glittering stones and call them jewels. And admire them because they are resplendent like the stars, and transparent like the air, and pellucid like the sea. But the stars themselves which are ten thousand times more useful, great, and glorious they disregard. Nor shall the air itself be counted anything, though it be worth all the pearls and diamonds in ten thousand worlds. A work of God so divine by reason of its precious and pure transparency, that all worlds would be nothing without such a treasure.

THOMAS TRAHERNE *c.* 1637–1674

7 *Cancer in the Heart*

There is an old story of a man who lived in a magnificent house in which both his father and his grandfather had died of cancer. He became convinced that the germs of the disease must be lurking in the timbers of the house. He had it pulled down and in its place had a new and costly building erected. In this new house, not long after, he died of cancer. The disease was in the man and not in the building.

We hear sometimes of how men are going to build a brave new world in which the diseases of poverty, insecurity, war, crimes and all the other ugly cancers which eat at the heart of a healthy society are to be eliminated. In this new world, economic planning, welfare states, United Nations, and universal education will bring this about. Unfortunately this is far from the truth. The cancer does not lie in the materials which go to make up society. It lies in the hearts of human beings. It is only by tearing out the cancer of evil from men's hearts that a new and healthy world can be built.

8 *Eternity*

Sometimes people say that they cannot understand that they won't be bored with all eternity at their command in Heaven. This denotes a complete misunderstanding of the nature of eternity. In Heaven there is no 'before and after' in our sense of the words. We will no longer be creatures of time. Time has no meaning when one is united to God who is eternal. He is the 'Alpha and the Omega' and 'The beginning and the end' of all existence. All eternity will be seen as one moment of complete and perfect happiness. We will live permanently in the present. No longer will we see 'In a dark mannner as in a mirror' but we will see God 'face to face' in all His splendour and glory. We shall 'know even as we are known'. This will absorb our whole being. Even our human love which we will still have for others will be experienced in the light of God's infinite love.

9 *Expectancy*

One of the pleasant memories of my boyhood was the visit to the theatre in the holidays. In those days this was a great occasion. And one of the keenest moments of enjoyment was just before the curtain went up – that moment when the lights in the auditorium were dimmed – when conversation died down – the orchestra tuned up and the curtain gave a preliminary sway. Before any exciting event there is this joy of expectancy. It is this joy of expectancy that Christians experience in Advent and give voice to in their prayers. For they are waiting for the curtain to rise on a magnificent drama in which the glory of the Lord will be revealed and the whole world stage flooded with transforming light. In that Light they will see light. For the feast of Christmas celebrates the coming of God into His creation transforming it by His presence and giving it a completely new dimension.

10 *Prayer*

If thou shouldst never see my face again
Pray for my soul. More things are wrought by prayer
Than this world dreams of. Wherefore, let thy voice
Rise like a fountain for me night and day.
For what are men better than sheep or goats
That nourish a blind life within the brain,
If, knowing God, they lift not hands in prayer
Both for themselves and those who call them friend?
For so the whole round world is every way
Bound by gold chains about the feet of God.

The Passing of Arthur
ALFRED LORD TENNYSON 1809–1892

11 *The Watch*

Rosini was once given a watch by the King of France. He had had it for some time when a friend said to him: 'You don't know the full value of that watch.' 'Why do you say that?' asked Rosini. 'I know it is a valuable watch.' 'Lend it to me,' said his friend who took the watch and pressed a secret spring in it; part of the watch flew open revealing a beautiful little miniature of Rosini himself. He had had the watch for some time without knowing what it contained. We often do the same in regard to God's word in Scripture. We read it casually but we don't press the secret spring which will reveal its hidden treasure of truth. We need to approach it with prayer and devotion if we are to release the spring.

12 *The Unseen in the Seen*

St Paul wrote to the Corinthians: 'We look not at the things which are seen but at the things which are not seen; for the things which are seen are temporal but the things which are unseen are eternal.'

At first sight, if taken literally, these words seem to mean that we should look upon things in this world as a kind of unfortunate necessity, as stumbling blocks on our way to the next world. In other words that we should look upon this world as unimportant. This would of course be completely to misunderstand what Paul is saying. He is telling us that we should have the vision to see this world in terms of the next. The visible should not act as a screen to the invisible but as a means of getting in touch with it. It is only through the seen that we can get in touch with the unseen. We can indeed enjoy the good things of this world but they must not blind our vision to the good things of the next.

13 *A Game of Chess*

Suppose it was perfectly certain that the life and fortune of everyone of us would, one day or other, depend upon our winning or losing a game of chess. Don't you think that we should all consider it to be a primary duty to learn at least the names and moves of the pieces; to have a notion of gambit, and a keen eye for all the means of giving and getting out of check? Do you not think that we should look with a disapprobation amounting to scorn, upon the father who allowed his son, or the state which allowing its members to grow up without knowing a pawn from a knight?

Yet it is a very plain and elementary truth, that the life, the fortune, and the happiness of every one of us, and more or less, of those who are connected with us, do depend upon our knowing something of the rules of a game infinitely more difficult and complicated than chess. It is a game that has been played for untold ages, every man and woman of us being one of the two players in a game of his or her own. The chess board is the world, the pieces are the phenomena of the universe, the rules of the game are what we call the laws of Nature. The player on the other side is hidden from us. We know that His play is always fair, just and patient. But also we know to our cost, that He never overlooks a mistake, or makes the slightest allowance for ignorance. To the man who plays well, the highest stakes are paid. And one who plays ill is checkmated – without haste, but without remorse.

THOMAS HENRY HUXLEY 1825–1895

14 *The Golden Journey*

We are the pilgrims, Master, we shall go
Always a little further; it may be
Beyond that last blue mountain barred with snow
Across that angry or that glimmering sea.
While on a throne or guarded in a cave
There lives a prophet who can understand
Why men were born; but surely we are brave
Who take the Golden Road to Samarkand.

JAMES ELROY FLECKER 1884–1915

15 *Augustine robs an Orchard*

Yet the sin he regrets most bitterly was nothing more dreadful than the robbing of an orchard. Pears he had in plenty, none the less he went, with a band of roisterers, and pillaged another man's pear tree. 'I loved the sin, not that which I obtained by the same, but I loved the sin itself.' There lay the sting in it. They were not even unusually excellent pears. 'A pear tree there was, near our vineyard, heavy laden with fruit, which tempted not greatly either the sight or taste. To the shaking and robbing thereof certain most wicked youths (whereof I was one) went late one night. We carried away huge burdens of fruit from thence, not for our own eating, but to be cast before the hogs.'

Oh, moonlight night of Africa, and orchard by those wild sea banks where once Dido stood; oh, laughter of boys among the shaken leaves, and sound of falling fruit; how do you live alone out of so many nights that no man can remember? For Carthage is destroyed, in deed, and forsaken of the sea, yet that one hour of summer is to be unforgotten while man has memory of the life story of his past.

ANDREW LANG 1844–1912

16 *The Pilgrimage*

Give me my scallop-shell of quiet,
My staff of faith to walk upon,
My scrip of joy, immortal diet,
My bottle of salvation,
My gown of glory, hope's true gage;
And thus I'll take my pilgrimage

Blood must be my body's balmer;
No other balm will there be given;
Whilst my soul, like quiet palmer,
Travelleth towards the land of heaven;
Over the silver mountains,
Where spring the nectar fountains:
   There will I kiss
   The bowl of bliss;
And drink my everlasting fill
Upon every milken hill.
My soul will be a-dry before;
But after, it will thirst no more.

SIR WALTER RALEIGH 1552–1618

17 *John the Baptist*

The last and greatest Herald of Heaven's King,
Girt with rough skins, hies to the deserts wild,
Among that savage broad the woods forth bring,
Which He than man more harmless friend and mild.
His food was locusts, and what young doth spring
With honey that from the virgin hives distilled;
Parched body, hollow eyes, some uncouth thing
Made Him appear, long since from earth exiled.
There burst He forth; 'All ye, whose hopes rely
On God, with Me amidst these deserts mourn;
Repent, repent, and from old errors turn!'
Who listened to His voice, obeyed His cry?
Only the echoes, which He made relent,
Rising from their marble caves 'Repent! Repent!'
WILLIAM DRUMMAND OF HAWTHORNDEN 1585–1649

18 *God dawned on Chaos*

Through wood and stream and field and hill and ocean
A quickening life from the Earth's heart has burst
As it has ever done, with change and motion,
From the great morning of the world when first
God dawned on Chaos; in its stream immersed,
The lamps of Heaven flash with a softer light;
All baser things pant with life's sacred thirst;
Diffuse themselves; and spend in love's delight
The beauty and the joy of their renewed might.
PERCY BYSSHE SHELLEY 1792–1822

19 *Prayer and Anger*

The first thing that hinders the prayer of a good man from obtaining its effects is a violent anger, and a violent storm in the spirit of him who prays ... Anger is a perfect alienation of the mind from prayer, and therefore is contrary to that attention which presents our prayers in a right line to God. For so I have seen a lark rising from his bed of grass and soaring upwards, singing as he rises, and hopes to get to Heaven, and climb above the clouds; but the poor bird was beaten back with the loud sighings of an eastern wind, and his motion made irregular and inconstant, descending more at every breath of the tempest, than it could recover by the liberation and frequent weighing of its wings; till the little creature was forced to sit down and pant, and stay till the storm was over; and then it made a prosperous flight, and did rise and sing, as if it had learned music and motion from an angel as he passed sometime through the air about his ministries here below: so the prayer of a good man.

JEREMY TAYLOR 1613–1667

20 *God's Grandeur*

The world is charged with the grandeur of God.
It will flame out, like shining from shook foil;
It gathers to a greatness, like the ooze of oil
Crushed. Why do men then now not reck His rod?
Generations have trod, have trod, have trod;
And all is seared with trade; bleared, smeared with toil,
And wears man's smudge and shares man's smell: the
   soil

Is bare now, nor can foot feel, being shod.
And for all this, Nature is never spent;
There lives the dearest freshness deep down things;
And though the last lights off the black west went
Oh, morning, at the brown brink eastward springs –
Becuse the Holy Ghost over the bent
World broods with warm breast and with ah! bright
    wings.

GERARD MANLEY HOPKINS 1844–1889

21 *An Apotheosis of Matter*

On 6 August 1945, Hiroshima was reduced to ruins by an atom bomb. Ten years later the first hydrogen bomb was exploded. Ever since those days the shadow of the mushroom cloud has hung sombre and menacing over the world. The bomb is the apotheosis of matter – its victory over the human spirit. It is a moloch more deadly than any of the imaginary gods of paganism, a veritable Frankenstein, an ugly technological monster that may at any time break out of its confinement to devour its creator. Sheer materialism, whatever its form, degrades humanity. Human beings are composed of matter and spirit and the balance between them must be maintained if they are not to dehumanise themselves. Man's material needs must be directed by those of his spirit. Man needs the Spirit of God to inspire his human spirit to direct his energies in the right direction. If he allows love of things to stifle his spirit he is destroying his true humanity.

22 *The Mirror*

St Paul speaks of this world as a mirror in which objects are reflected in a confused and indistinct manner. We cannot see the complete reality, only faint images flit across our vision. Cardinal Newman wrote: 'In spite of this universal which we see, there is another world, quite as far-spreading, quite as close to us, and more wonderful; another world all around us, though we see it not, and more wonderful than the world we see.'

The reflections in the world mirror give us only faint intimations of this other world, a world far more substantial and lasting than the one we tread on. The pageant and play of nature do indeed reflect the beauty and power and glory of their artist and creator but at the same time they act as a screen preventing the direct vision of him. The person of faith can say in the words of Francis Thompson:

> O world invisible, we view Thee,
> O world intangible, we touch Thee,
> O world unknowable, we know Thee,
> Inapprehensible, we clutch Thee.

23 *Christmas Prayer*

Loving Father, help us to remember the birth of Jesus, that we may share in the song of the angels, the gladness of the shepherds, and the wisdom of the wise men. Close the door of hate and open the door of love all over the world. Let kindness come with every gift and good desires with every greeting. Deliver us from evil by the blessing which

Christ brings, and teach us to be merry with clean hearts. May the Christmas morning make us happy to be Thy children and the Christmas evening bring us to our beds with grateful thoughts, forgiving and forgiving for Jesus' sake. Amen.

ROBERT LOUIS STEVENSON 1850–1894

24 *Christmas Eve*

On Christmas Eve the bells were rung;
On Christmas Eve the mass was sung;
That only night, in all the year,
Saw the stoled priest the chalice rear.
The damsel donned her kirtle sheen;
The hall was dressed with holly green;
Forth to the wood did merry-men go,
To gather in the mistletoe.
Then opened wide the Baron's hall;
Power laid his rod of rule aside,
And ceremony doffed his pride.

The heir, with roses in her shoes,
That night might village partners choose.
The lord, underogating, share
The vulgar game of 'post and pair'.
All hailed with uncontrolled delight,
And general voice, the happy night,
That to the cottage, as the crown,
Brought tidings of salvation down.

Marmion SIR WALTER SCOTT 1771–1832

25 *The Burning Babe*

As I in hoary Winter's night stood shivering in the snow,
Surprised I was with sudden heat which made my heart
    to glow;
And lifting up a fearful eye to view what fire was near,
A pretty babe all burning bright did in the air appear;
Who, scorchd with excessive heat such floods of tears
    did shed,
As though his floods should quench his flames which
    with his tears were fed.

'Alas!' quoth he, 'but newly born in fiery heats I fry,
Yet none approach to warm their hearts or feel my fire
    but I!
My faultless breast the furnace is, the fuel wounding
    thorns;
Love is the fire, and sighs the smoke, the ashes shame
    and scorns;
The fuel Justice layeth on, and Mercy blows the coals;
The metal in this furnace wrought are men's defiléd
    souls.
For which, as now on fire I am, to work them to their
    good,
So will I melt into a bath to wash them in my blood.'
With this he vanished out of sight and swiftly shrunk
    away,
And straight I calléd into mind that it was Christmas
    Day.

ROBERT SOUTHWELL 1561–1595

26 *Seed Time and Harvest*

There is a time of weeping and there is a time of laughing. But as you see, He setteth the weeping time before, for that is the time of this wretched world and the laughing time shall come after in Heaven. There is also a time of sowing, and a time of reaping too. Now must we in this world sow, that in the other world reap: and in this short sowing time of this weeping world, must we water our seed with the showers of our tears, and then shall we have in Heaven a merry laughing harvest for ever.

A Dialogue of Comfort in Tribulation
SIR THOMAS MORE 1477–1535

27 *Religion and Gloom*

There are some people who look upon religion as a gloomy affair. They seem to think that those who live lives for God 'must scorn delights and live laborious days', that they must reply in the affirmative to Sir Toby Belch's question: 'Dost thou think because thou are virtuous there will be no more cakes and ale?' Is it really conducive to one's spiritual health always to chew the pills administered by the stern matron, life? Is one's ideal to be that of the monk in Byron's poem:

> Deep in that cell Honorious long did dwell
> In hope to merit Heaven by making earth a Hell?

The answer is, of course, that this attiude is nonsensical. Christianity would be a cold and barren affair if it were true and it would soon have few adherents. One must remember that mortification, suffering, pain have no spiritual value in themselves. It is one's motive that decides their merit or lack of it. Judged by themselves our pleasures and joys can be just as meritorious as our sufferings. The reason why the latter are likely to be more meritorious is that there will be less of self in them when accepted out of love for God.

28 *Joy and Pain*

The Greeks had a saying that 'the gods sell us all the good things that they give us', that is they give us nothing good that we don't buy at the cost of some evil. Socrates said that some god tried to mix in one lump pain and pleasure but that, unable to succeed, he besought to couple them at least by the tail. Life is a mixture of pain and joy, of fortune and misfortune, of happiness and sadness, of failure and success. It has, as the saying has it, 'Ups and downs'. Normally one does not start at the top of the ladder of life – one begins with great toil to work one's way up from the bottom. Success is often achieved while mounting rungs of failures and misfortunes. At the beginning of the world, God said to Adam and Eve 'in the sweat of thy brow thou shalt eat bread'. This has been true of the vast number of the human race. Neither success or happiness comes without, not only struggle, but pain of some kind. The recognition of this fact can itself be a help in life.

29 *Holy Sonnet*

At the round earth's imagined corners, blow
Your trumpets, Angels, and arise, arise
From death, you numberless infinities
Of souls, and to your scattered bodies go,
All whom the flood did, and fire shall o'erthrow,
All whom war, dearth, age, agues, tyrannies,
Despair, law, chance, hath slain, and you whose eyes
Shall behold God and never taste death's woe.
But let them sleep, Lord, and me mourn a space,
For if above all these my sins abound,
'Tis late to ask abundance of Thy grace,
When we are there; here on this lowly ground,
Teach me how to repent; for that's as good
As if Thou hadst seal'd my pardon with Thy blood.

JOHN DONNE 1573–1631

30 *The Broken Statue*

An American company of soldiers going into a bombed town in France during the last great war came across a broken statue of Christ lying on the ground. Some Christians among them gathered the broken pieces and fastened them together but they could not find the hands. So someone wrote on a placard: 'We are his hands' and hung it on the restored statue. The same sentiments are expressed by an anonymous writer: 'The only hands and feet God has in this world are our hands and feet.'

31 *Resurrection and Life*

The fall doth pass the rise is worth;
For both hath in itself the germ of death,
But death hath in itself the germ of birth.
It is the falling acorn buds the tree,
The falling rain that bears the greenery,
The fern plants moulder when the ferns arise.
For there is nothing lives but something dies,
And there is nothing dies but something lives,
Till the skies be fugitives,
Till time, the hidden root of change updries
Are Birth and Death inseparable on earth;
For they are twain yet one, and Death is Birth.

FRANCIS THOMPSON 1859–1907

Index